Living Your Best

A Powerful Blueprint
for Personal Transformation

Steven Smith, Ph.D.

Living Your Best: A Powerful Blueprint
for Personal Transformation

StevenSmith-author.com

Copyright © 2012 Steven Smith, Ph.D.

Wisdom of the Heart, Inc.

Lexington, KY

ISBN: 0-615-61162-1

ISBN-13: 978-0-615-61162-4

LCCN: 2012901527

*dedicated to those kindred
souls striving to be their best*

ACKNOWLEDGMENTS

So many friends and teachers in my life have left their fingerprints on this book. I am deeply grateful for their assistance and their unique contributions to my personal journey. Some have had such profound impacts I would be remiss in not giving them due acknowledgment.

I would first like to thank my loving wife, Janet, who has consistently encouraged and supported my efforts to articulate that which resonates so deeply within me. Her generous gift of time and love have provided me with the opportunity to complete this work.

My mother's spiritual conviction and her tireless search for truth has served as an invaluable beacon to guide me through the labyrinth of life. Clarice's courage and integrity have shown me it is indeed possible to be a divine human.

The balanced nature of my father, J.B., has always provided me with stability during difficult times. His gentle and accepting nature has been a positive example for me throughout my life.

Being a father to my two sons has afforded me many lessons that have stimulated my growth over the years. Jared and Jordan have helped to shape my life in new and rich ways I could never before have imagined, and I am very grateful for that.

Many thanks go to those who provided invaluable help with excellent editing suggestions: Regi Goffinet, Suzie Stammer, Karen

Miyares, Vicky Broadus, Janet Smith, Jayne Treadwell, Clarice O'Bryan, Shan Borchers, Deborah Raad, Lakshmi Sriraman, Lea Schultz, Irmgard Huddy, and David Sefton. I am deeply indebted for their contributions to this work.

Last but not least, I could not have written this book without my spiritual family. For eighteen years they have been an oasis of support, wisdom, and friendship. They are a huge part of my heart and I love them dearly. In particular I am forever grateful to Lea Schultz for her many beautiful teachings that are generously sprinkled throughout this book.

To all of you I say—thank you!

CONTENTS

THE FIVE PRINCIPLES

INTEGRATING THE PRINCIPLES

PREFACE

Life—what an amazing adventure! It's a journey rich with reward, providing breathtakingly beautiful moments and loving experiences. It's also incredibly challenging. In spite of our best efforts, dodging life's many potholes is a tricky business at best and can result in tragic experiences, giving rise to hopelessness and despair.

Each of us shares a deep longing to experience positive emotions, to have healthy relationships, and to feel engaged in life. These are key factors in our well-being.[1] But life doesn't come with a built-in navigation system. How do we cultivate these vital aspects of a good and happy life? What are the steps we can take to create a foundation that enables us to live our best?

I'm very excited to share with you some powerful tools that will help you create that foundation. The principles in this book have profoundly transformed my life and I'm confident they will transform yours as well. You deserve to have a life you love, and the good news is you can create it!

My sincerest wish is that the teachings and tools within this book will open a personal doorway for you. May that doorway lead to the emergence of a most delightful version of you.

MY IMPETUS FOR CHANGE

We all wish to be happy. As a practicing psychologist for 35 years, I have been privileged to work with hundreds of people attempting to bring order to the immense complexity of their lives. It has truly been an honor to serve others in this way.

While my study of psychology has certainly been advantageous in helping me manage my own life, I am in no way immune to the many challenges of being human, for each of us is an unfinished creation. Learning as we go, we gain knowledge through our individual experiences.

Sometimes events and circumstances come together in a way that practically compels us to take the next step in our personal development. Such was the case for me, which eventually led to the writing of this book. Knee deep in some personal ruts, there were a series of catalysts which forced me to look at stagnating patterns in my life that were no longer working.

The first of those catalysts occurred one day when I came upon a group of Buddhist monks at a local mall. Their work spanning the course of several days, they were completing a mandala— a very intricate design in colored sand. It was a beautiful act of unity, with each monk making a personal contribution to the stunning work of art.

After they finished their project and allowed everyone time to admire their work, I was startled to see the monks suddenly scatter the sand, releasing their attachment to what they had created. Profoundly impacted by their actions, I wanted to reach out and stop them. I didn't understand creating something so beautiful if it was to be scrapped in the end.

Although I didn't realize it at the time, my reaction to the mandala's destruction reflected a strongly held belief that my sought after destinations were far more important than my process of getting there. It also revealed a consistent pattern in my life of becoming attached to my creations by identifying with them.

As an American male, I was trained to strive for accomplishments, not to savor the steps I took to get there. I had learned the lessons of my capitalistic culture well and had come to believe a life must be full to be fulfilling—in other words, the more accomplishments, possessions, or experiences I had, the happier I would be. There was a problem: it wasn't true. Stretched far beyond what was healthy, my life was not in balance. I no longer had passion for parts of my life that had nurtured me in the past, yet I struggled to let them go.

In stark contrast, these engaging and joyful monks didn't identify with the mandala. They were living examples of nonattachment to their creations, seemingly just as happy dismantling the mandala as they were creating it. I longed for that experience.

Shortly after my encounter with the monks, a second defining event unfolded in the form of an insightful dream where I was walking down a narrow path, struggling to hold as many rocks as I could possibly carry. Cradling them with my arms, I was laboring mightily under their weight, resolute in my determination not to let any of them drop.

Most of my dreams don't make much sense to me, but I didn't need an analyst for this one. The symbols were clear. My lifelong tendency to crowd as much into a given day as possible was taking its toll. My life had become bloated with far too many activities and commitments. With happiness becoming more elusive, I increasingly felt like a human *doing*, not a human *being*. Others had labeled me a poster child for American success with a great family, career, health, and home. But something was missing and I knew it.

The urge from within to find greater peace and balance in my life received one final push. Little did I know that it would come gift-wrapped in yet another dream—a nightmare that left me awash in a cold sweat. Someone in my dream was holding me underwater and each time I came up for air, I was submerged again as I furiously struggled for my life. Who would want to do this terrible thing to me?

At first the face of the perpetrator was blurred but eventually I caught a glimpse of this despicable person—it was me! *I* was the person holding down the highest part of me that was desperately gasping for expression in my life. I had become an accomplished human in the eyes of the world but had lost the sacredness and joy of living. I was missing the miracle of life as it unfolded in each moment.

When I awoke, the choices in front of me were crystal-clear. I could continue my familiar patterns, allowing this precious life to pass me by, or I could step off the cliff of what was known to me and recreate the game board of my life. My greater self beckoned me to choose the latter—and I did.

I began by asking for help, which was never my strong suit. Imploring the Universe to work with me, I made a commitment to release *anything* that was getting in the way of my happiness and peace. There would be no sacred cows. I was willing to let go of unfulfilling relationships, activities, material possessions—whatever was needed to align my life with greater well-being. I knew what *wasn't* working but had no idea what steps I should take going forward.

I don't remember how long it took, but help came. Not as a booming voice from heaven or even as a tiny whisper. Instead, it came in the form of a thought—a *principle* that became my mantra for the next nine months. The symbolism of that period was not lost on me; I was literally birthing a new version of me by aligning my life with this principle. It was a powerful doorway to the first step in my transformation.

As I increasingly incorporated this principle into my life, the internal and external changes were unmistakable. I was astonished by the enormous impact aligning my thoughts with this single principle had on my life. I found myself responding quite positively to people and situations that had previously created significant stress within me.

More help came. The process of unfolding principles would continue for the next few months until there were a total of five, each building upon the previous one. I was both amazed and delighted by their powerful impact for they profoundly changed my experience of life.

These Five Principles, as I came to call them, didn't come *from* me as much as they came *to* me. They brought much-needed balance to my life and became a template through which I filtered the events of each day. Incorporating them did not require that I meditate for long periods, change my job, or make any radical external changes—it required rewiring my thought patterns. Whether I was in bed, in the shower, or driving to work, I focused several times a day on each principle, opening myself to embody the essence of each.

Working with them changed me on the inside. Figuratively it was like changing my sunglasses from gray lenses to amber ones. I was looking at the same world, but everything seemed different—because I was.

USING THIS BOOK

This book is divided into two major sections. The first is an overview of the Five Principles. It explores each principle in detail and fleshes out some important and relevant aspects of each.

The second section of this book is a guide for integrating the Five Principles into your life—moving them from philosophy to practicality, from thought to action. Many self-help books excel at telling you what your problems are and what you should do differently; they often fall woefully short in telling you *how* to make those changes. To that end I have created a rich set of tools specifically designed to help you make the Five Principles an integral part of your life.

Because of their breadth and scope, there are a multitude of ways to interpret the principles. The various aspects of each that I address in this book are far from exhaustive. Please don't limit yourself to *my* interpretation of them. Your understanding of the principles will broaden as you work with them and discover how they improve your life. Take what works for you and give yourself the freedom to interpret them in ways that make them truly yours.

INTRODUCTION TO THE
FIVE PRINCIPLES

The Five Principles offer a pathway for functioning at your best regardless of race, gender, religion, class, or personality type. They work in relationships, business settings, and families. Because they encourage many positive behaviors, qualities, and time-honored virtues, they fit easily into most religious and spiritual paradigms. The principles are consistent with a Christian emphasis on living a loving life, Buddhist principles of detachment, Hindu principles of honoring the sacredness of life, and a Judaic and Islamic emphasis on serving God.

The Five Principles are a pathway that restructures us on the inside so loving behavior becomes our outer expression.

The Five Principles are a roadmap for creating a life of greater emotional balance and well-being. If you suffer from anxiety and depression, utilizing the principles will help you to gain control over them. If you worry excessively over things you can't control or if you lose your temper quicker than you would like, using the principles will help you to make positive changes. If you're controlling, judgmental, or unhappy, they will bring you much-needed relief.

The Five Principles are universal in their applications and are grounded in wisdom that transcends the ages. This book provides a distillation of these teachings into a succinct and easy-to-remember format that is very unique. It's a powerful blueprint for personal transformation that teaches you to align your thoughts and behaviors with the very best part of you.

The principles might seem deceptively simple at first glance, but they are practical and profound in their everyday applications. Simply reading about these principles won't bring you the change you desire, but applying them will. Please give yourself the time to work with them. You'll be amazed by the positive changes they can bring to your life.

THE FIVE PRINCIPLES

THE FIRST PRINCIPLE

Nothing Has to Happen My Way

Nothing has to happen

. . . the way *I wish it would*

. . . the way *I think it should*

. . . the way *I expect it to*

. . . the way *I want it to*

. . . *when I want*

. . . *with whom I want*

. . . any *differently than it is right now*

for me to be at peace.

I had asked for help and it had come in the form of the First Principle. There was no denying the irrefutable truth of it. Nothing *had* to happen, nor did it have to happen *my way*, for me to be at peace.

It was an epiphany to realize I had never been upset in life except when things weren't going the way I wanted. Although I was well versed in numerous teachings on acceptance, never before had a singular thought struck at the very heart of what created almost all the stress in my life: my need to be in control. Despite being a psychologist, I had never come to the remarkable truth that virtually every negative emotion I had ever experienced resulted from my *needing the present to be different than it was.* This recognition hit me like a bus! Could it really be that simple? How could this fundamental truth have escaped me all my life?

The implications of this realization were far-reaching. If I were to fully embrace this principle, there would be no room for the many "shoulds" that often gave rise to my expectation and judgment. As long as my sense of peace depended on something happening the way I thought it *should* have happened or someone doing what I thought they *should* have been doing, my well-being was at the mercy of external events. I could no longer hide behind the false belief that other people or situations were responsible for my happiness or lack of it.

My complaints would have to go. I began to see just how crazy it was to complain about anything! When I complained I was taking issue with reality for not matching up with what I wanted it to be. It was as ludicrous as looking at a maple tree and being critical that it wasn't a willow. Incorporating the First Principle meant my complaining had to stop.

It also meant releasing my old friend—entitlement, who had shown up many times in my life. The First Principle showed me I was *entitled* to absolutely nothing. Life was rich and filled with opportunities for growth, but it didn't owe me anything. A goodbye kiss from my wife, respect from others, financial security—these were desired outcomes, but not things I was entitled to receive.

Resentment, anger, frustration, worry, controlling behavior— the First Principle offered me a key to extricate myself from these imprisoning emotions. The potential payoff for adopting this principle was huge, but I knew implementing it would be a challenge.

Much of my human identity was based on setting goals and reaching them. Things had always needed to go according to plan—*my* plan. It seemed like heresy to believe I could be happy without investing myself in a particular outcome. But the First Principle intrigued me. It offered a promising pathway for detaching from things over which I had no control. It offered peace.

Resolute in my desire to walk a different path, I began to experiment by holding the phrase "nothing has to happen my way" in my mind as a guiding thought throughout the day. Changes in my experiences were fairly immediate. I was amazed to discover that my focus on a single thought could change my experience in such a profound way.

I noticed my anger toward myself and others declining rapidly. The same was true for all the inanimate objects of my anger: a broken belt on the lawnmower, a glass falling out of my hand and shattering on the floor, and the thousands of other things that refused to cooperate with how I wanted them to unfold in my life. It was incredibly emancipating to realize my anger was nothing more than a personal temper tantrum because reality wasn't lining up with my expectations, desires, or wants.

By detaching from that which was outside of my control, I began to open the door to a stranger in my life: acceptance. With every tiny victory of accepting what *was*, my controlling tendencies were losing their grip on me. Paradoxically, and to my pleasant surprise, I found that as I worked to let go of my need to control others, I felt increasingly in control of myself.

Life was easier and I was calmer, especially on the inside. By releasing my need for particular outcomes, peace blossomed in me where it had not previously existed. Those who were close to me noticed. It was a very welcomed change.

Nothing has to happen...*my* way. Don't be fooled—this is a deceptively powerful statement. It's a simple but great truth. Say it aloud. As you hear yourself say the words, you know they are true. The Universe does not revolve around you, not even in the slightest! If all your wants, dreams, and desires were to end because of your sudden death, virtually everything in the world would go on as it had before. That fact doesn't diminish your importance but rather points out the obvious: what you think needs to or should happen at any moment is nothing more than your personal desire.

At first glance this principle might seem ludicrous. Of course things have to happen. We have to pay our bills, we need to have jobs, we have to spend less than we make. The list goes on.

It's true. We all have responsibilities. However, the key phrase here is—*my way*—because it's our need to have things go our way that causes most of our imbalance and suffering.

But releasing our need to control is met with great resistance for our brains are hard-wired to keep us safe and alive. It does that by seeking to control the environment around us so we feel more secure. Letting go of our natural instinct to control our environment feels unsafe. Yet paradoxically, relinquishing control is a vital step toward greater peace and well-being in our lives.

The simple truth is that we can only control ourselves. When we attempt to exert control over another person or a situation in an effort to make ourselves feel more secure, we almost invariably guarantee a negative experience. By needing people to behave as we wish or situations to play out as we desire, we set up dysfunctional patterns that show up in three major ways.

Thinking people and situations should be as we desire which results in:

- ➢ blame
- ➢ resentment
- ➢ expectations
- ➢ judgment
- ➢ entitlement
- ➢ anger

Fearing people and situations will be different from what we desire which results in:

- ➢ obsession
- ➢ worry
- ➢ fear of change
- ➢ anxiety

Trying to force people and situations to be what we desire which results in:

- ➢ drama
- ➢ justification
- ➢ the need to be right
- ➢ abuse of power
- ➢ controlling behavior

"Nothing has to happen my way" can help you detach in a thousand different ways. It beckons you to purge the silly human minutia, the comparative judgment, the wishing that things were different from what they are, the rumination about why things weren't different in the past, and the fearful thinking about what might happen in the future.

This First Principle is a powerful statement that enables you to stand face to face with your humanness and say, "No, I will not let you rule me. No, I will not let my mind assume the worst and create fearful future scenarios. No, I will not focus on what is not working instead of what is. No, I will not keep myself unhappy with unmet expectations, assumptions, and comparative judgments."

It's very empowering when nothing has to happen your way for you're proclaiming you are bigger than anything outside of you that might derail your inner peace. And you are right—you are.

By aligning with what is, you release your resistance to the current reality and are escorted through the door of *detachment*. As you stop resisting the flow of life, you free yourself to experience greater peace and positivity.

> Each of The Five Principles bears many fruits. Following a general discussion of each principle, I will flesh out some important gifts and aspects of each that have helped me to develop a broader and richer understanding of them.

ACCEPTANCE

A great gift of the First Principle is acceptance. Acceptance flows from the awareness that there are a million different perspectives and paths in this world of free will. Often we become judgmental when something is different from what we think it should be. Yet our judgment of whether a situation is positive or negative is always a matter of personal perspective. An economic downturn might be bad for high-end clothing stores but a boon for those who sell used cars. Is the downturn a bad thing? It all depends on whom you ask.

Acceptance is not resignation, for it's possible to accept current circumstances while reaching for more. For example, you can accept your current job situation while knowing you want to make a change in the future. Keeping a foot in both camps, you continue working hard while sending out your resume to potential employers. Because you're not resisting your current job, complaining about it, or angry about it, you're free to use your energy in constructive ways to bring about a positive change. By aligning yourself with what *is,* you can create that delicate balance where you're planning for a positive future while not being unhappy about where you are now.

On the other hand, *tolerating* a situation that is unhealthy for you is not acceptance—it's avoidance. Fear is the usual culprit. For instance, consider the case of Tiffany, a single mother whose son of twenty-five years neither works nor goes to school, yet lives in her house and eats out of her refrigerator. Rather than setting clear boundaries that would give her son the choice of being responsible by going to work or to school, or leaving her home if he does neither, she avoids confronting the issue and allows his mooching to continue. Fearful he might end up homeless if she makes him leave, she is unwilling to force the issue.

When Tiffany is able to relinquish her need to control the outcome and can place the options squarely in front of her son, she takes the important step of no longer being responsible for him. Now the responsibility is his. To do that she has to be willing to accept the choice he makes and release her attempts to control the situation.

Accepting others by allowing them to be who they are, instead of trying to manipulate them so they are who we want them to be, is one of the hardest and most loving things we ever do. The First Principle makes this an easier process by offering an effective framework for cultivating acceptance.

Reflection

➤ Think of a situation in your life that is difficult for you to accept.

➤ What would you have to release to be more accepting in this area?

PRESENT-CENTEREDNESS

The best things in life happen *only* in the present. Belly laughter, savoring a delicious dish, stroking a tiny kitten, a brilliant orange sunset, an emotionally bonding sexual experience, or looking into the smiling face of an adoring infant—these moments touch our hearts and create loving connections. They give our lives meaning.

Yet we struggle with living in our present because it is so easy to be elsewhere. We have the amazing ability to move forward in time to plan, dream, and create. We can also shuffle through the pages of our pasts, not only remembering them but learning from them. These are powerful abilities—but as with any great power they can be misused.

It is vital that we learn to stop misusing our minds so they can work for us instead of against us.

One of the ways we misuse our minds is spending an inordinate amount of time focusing on negative aspects of our pasts. The past can imprison us for life. Perhaps we even feel justified in keeping a painful memory alive, having identified so strongly with it that we find it hard to let go. Unwittingly, keeping a painful past alive keeps us attached to that pain. By releasing daily the things that don't go our way and accepting that they don't have to, we prevent the negative emotions of regret, judgment, and blame from accumulating and cluttering our emotional inboxes.

We can also misuse our minds by worrying about our future, fearing it will not unfold in the ways we desire. We scare ourselves by allowing our brains to create Stephen King movies and then believing they're true because *we* created them. The irony, of course, is we are using the power of our thoughts to create the very anxiety and insecurity we are hoping to avoid. Eek!

The following chart is an illustration of our ability to use and misuse our minds with regard to time.

PAST	PRESENT	FUTURE
	YOUR POINT OF POWER	
HEALTHY USE OF MIND	Joy	HEALTHY USE OF MIND
Learning from past	Sound	Planning
Positive nostalgia	Sight	Dreaming
	Taste	Setting goals
MISUSE OF MIND	Touch	
Resentment	Smell	MISUSE OF MIND
Guilt	Laughter	Worry
Depression	Excitement	Fear
Anger	Creativity	Anxiety
Blame	Relaxation	Catastrophizing
Bitterness	Sexual experience	Pessimism
Lack of forgiveness	Love given	But what if...
Judgement of self	Love received	Fearful fantasies

Many people delude themselves into thinking that when they worry they will somehow keep a dreaded event at bay. Psychologists call this *magical thinking.* But worry is damaging, because your body is an equal-opportunity protector. It doesn't know the difference between real threats and false alarms. As long as you *think* a threat is real, your body reacts as though it is. If I come up behind you and put a ball point pen at your neck, tell you I've got a gun and you believe me, your body will react as if the threat were real. That's the power of thought.

"But," you might ask, "how can I *not* worry when a loved one is in pain? What if a good friend is in the hospital with lung cancer? I love my friend and of course I'll lose sleep and constantly fret about the outcome of his illness. How can I not worry?"

Separating worry from concern can be extremely helpful in challenging situations like this. Concern differs from worry because concerns *can be acted upon*. There are several ways to express concern for your friend who is in the hospital. You can go visit, say a prayer, send a card, cook a dish, or call to offer comfort. These are actions that can be expressed and allow you to support your loved one.

Worry, on the other hand, is an internal action that leaves you feeling powerless and scared. All worry is self-abuse. Fear is not your friend in this situation. Take back your power by refusing the temptation to fill your head with catastrophic scenarios.

When nothing has to happen a certain way, we don't feel the need to anticipate and obsess about the future. Nor are we compelled to ruminate about the past when things don't go as we might have wished. Instead, we find it easier to keep our focus centered on the present. This frees us from most of our self-created stresses such as worry and depression.

FLOWING WITH CHANGE

When I was in the sixth grade, my science teacher asked my class to name the only thing in the world that never changes. With perplexed looks on our faces, we scoured our worldly experience for an answer, but to no avail. Finally our exasperated teacher relented and with dramatic flair said, "It's *change*! The only

thing that will never change is that there will always be change."
It seemed profound then and still does—everything is constantly
changing.

We love change when it's something we choose. When it's
forced upon us and loss is our uninvited guest, it's much harder
to accept. Perhaps you loved to jog but no longer can because of
aching joints; maybe you adored cooking gourmet meals but now
can't stand on your feet for the time required; maybe your favorite
coffeehouse closed down or you lost an intimate relationship.

These situations are stressful, but it's not the change that
tires us mentally and physically—it's our resistance to it. We resist change because fear promptly steps in and reminds us that
our future, which is unknown to us, might be less desirable than
our familiar past. How can we possibly make peace with a major
physical injury that changes our future forever? What if our new
job is less satisfying and less secure than the last one? How will
we manage the loneliness that comes from a breakup?

---

*We feel in control when we can
predict the future. That makes
unforeseen change the enemy.*

Most of the time when uninvited change comes into our lives,
we experience it as a loss rather than an opportunity. One of my
favorite sayings is, "When one door closes, another one opens—
but it's hell in the hallway." And sometimes it truly is, at least for
a while.

This was certainly true for me in my late twenties. I was an accomplished clog dancer and even won a national clogging championship. Clogging is an invigorating Appalachian percussive dance that can be done solo or with others, traditionally to lively fiddle tunes. As an instructor, I was well-known and taught this dance form both nationally and internationally. Clogging was a very big part of my adult life and provided me with many enduring friendships.

I shared my love for this dance form with thousands of others for almost twenty years. Then one day my world came crashing down: I suffered a knee injury that would suspend my dancing for years. I was devastated.

When that unwelcome change came to me, I had two choices— I could resist it or work with it. I chose to resist. I was not prepared psychologically for such a life-changing injury and subsequently went through a deep depression.

Resisting was very painful and frightening. I was unable to accept the injury or entertain the possibility of new opportunities. It was many months later, after much personal anguish, that I finally came to see the gifts of that experience and the new doors it had opened for me. I had lost my ability to dance, one of my most treasured ways of functioning in the world, but I eventually discovered there were other rich avenues to explore. Writing this book was one of them.

My ordeal taught me to trust that the Universe would always provide me with new possibilities when unwanted change came my way. The only requirement for taking advantage of that help was to accept what *was*, so I could open myself to those new possibilities.

The First Principle is a soothing elixir for the part of us that believes our security rests on things staying the same in our lives. They never do.

Reflection

➤ What unwelcome change have you experienced recently?

➤ Did you resist the change or flow with it? What could you have done to make it an easier process?

RELEASING EXPECTATIONS

You should. They should. I should. We should. Welcome to Shouldville, where reality rarely matches expectation. Take a moment and reflect on the negative emotions you've experienced in the past week. You might be surprised by how many were the result of unmet expectations.

Expectations are based on how we want the world and the people in it to treat us. It's not simply that we *desire* a particular outcome—it's that we're *invested* in things turning out a certain way. Expectations about how others should treat us, how we're going to feel, what we're going to experience—all set us up for resentment and blame when our expectations are not met.

The only time an expectation is valid is when it's based on an agreement you have with another person. If friends tell you they'll pick you up at six o'clock, you have a reasonable expectation they'll do so. Outside of such an agreement, expectations create obstacles that inevitably trip us up.

The First Principle taught me that expectations were my single biggest source of disappointment. Some of my expectations were quite obvious and ready to be plucked from my life. Others were much more insidious and sneaky. For example, I once gave someone a gift with no awareness I had any expectations attached. Only later, when I felt disappointed that their response was not what I had hoped it would be, did I recognize I had an expectation that went unmet.

"Nothing has to happen my way" is a powerful principle for extinguishing the flames that fuel our expectations.

FLEXIBILITY

We all desire certain outcomes. We make plans and set goals with the intent and purpose of making them a reality. However, stuff happens! Things break, people don't keep their commitments to us, we get sick—many things can thwart our best-laid plans. When that happens, we're faced with the task of creating something different from what we had originally intended. It's an opportunity to be flexible—or not, and our experience is almost totally dependent on which choice we make.

These choices can be illustrated with a fairly common scenario. Imagine two people, John and Diana, who get to the airport and find out their flight has been cancelled. Upon hearing of the cancellation, John is immediately overwhelmed with anxiety.

"Oh my God," he says, "I'm going to miss my meeting. This is terrible!" He runs to the ticket counter and harasses the attendant, saying his meeting simply cannot be missed. As the airline clerk scans the computer for available flights, John turns around and, in a voice seething with anger, says to the person behind him, "Can you believe the airlines? This is absolutely ridiculous!" John's drama will likely persist for some time—as will his churning stomach. It's a typical reaction for John when things don't go his way.

In the same predicament, Diana winces at the initial news of the cancellation. Taking a deep breath, she reminds herself that nothing has to happen her way. As she reaches the counter, instead of rebuking the airline clerk, she makes light conversation and comments on how difficult it must be for airline personnel to reschedule flights for their passengers. The clerk manages a smile and seems grateful for Diana's compassion. Diana's disappointment begins to subside as she makes a conscious effort to make the best of an undesirable situation.

Both John and Diana are eventually rerouted, but each created a very different experience. The quality of their experiences had nothing to do with what happened to them. It had *everything* to do with how they chose to respond.

Being flexible is tying your shoelace together when it breaks or making a quick batch of cookies when your cake flops. In short it's making the best of any given situation. Asking the question, "What is needed now?" will often enable you to tap into your creativity and inner wisdom to bring about the best workable outcome.

It's fine to have a plan for each day, but flexibility allows you to adjust on the fly and reset your course whenever outside forces alter it. Flexibility allows you to adapt when needed—to flow *with* your current circumstances rather than resist unforeseen changes in your plans.

Although the Five Principles build upon one another, *the First Principle is the kingpin.* Until we let go of the many ways we need the world to be different than it is, and as long as we seek to control others and situations so life happens our way, it will be next to impossible to incorporate the four principles that follow.

By releasing our need to control, in all its many shapes and guises, we create the conditions for true personal empowerment to flourish within us. When we are not ruled by the tyranny of the past or fear of the future, we open the doorway to real freedom in our lives. We make it possible to be at our best and to make the best possible choices in our present.

That's when it starts to be fun and what the next four principles are all about!

FIRST PRINCIPLE AFFIRMATION

Nothing Has to Happen My Way

Wherever I go and whatever I do today, I choose to accept my current reality and to work with it to bring about the highest and best outcome. I take comfort in knowing nothing has to happen my way for me to be at peace.

I am grateful for this day and for the gifts that this day will bring me—whether they are easy-to-accept gifts or challenges. I accept what is and allow it without resistance.

I release my expectations and my assumptions. I choose to be in the present moment and am empowered by knowing that my well-being is not determined by what is happening around me.

I take responsibility for creating peace within me and embrace my ability to adapt and be flexible in situations where it is needed.

I seek to empower, rather than disempower others, and to be mindful of situations where my power can be misused.

I open myself to accepting what I cannot change and release my need for anything to be different from the way it is.

I choose to see what is right and good in every situation—rather than what is not.

THE SECOND PRINCIPLE

Everything Matters

A stone tossed into a lake not only creates ripples that we see, but eventually goes on to touch the shoreline that we can't. Every action has a consequence, even though we may not see its immediate ramifications.

Imagine a decorative mobile hanging by a single thread. Its many pieces have been carefully constructed so the entire creation is balanced. If you were to take a penny from your pocket, you would be hard-pressed to find a spot on the mobile where you could add the penny without changing the original structure.

We each function as the penny. Everything we do affects our world. Each and every moment provides an opportunity to choose what we think, what we say, and what we do. That's why our actions matter so much. When we realize the importance of our actions, we become aware of the power we have to influence our world positively by making conscious choices to do the best we can, where we are at the time.

One day I had the good fortune to hear from a former client about the positive difference our work together had made in her life. She shared that she had eventually recovered from her depression and was now managing a health agency. Previously unable to even imagine being able to hold a job, now she was supervising and mentoring healthcare professionals who in turn provided needed services to the public at large.

This was a powerful epiphany for me, helping me to better understand the enormous influence we each have when we choose loving action. We never know when touching the life of one person will potentially touch the lives of many others. One positive action can change the world in a very big way because it can be paid forward many times.

Because we are each a part of the whole, everything we do affects the whole. Everything we do has an impact. Can you grasp the enormity of that? Just as one very small virus can affect the health of the entire physical body, choices in our lives—which may seem relatively inconsequential at the time—can have huge repercussions.

We each matter because as we transform, so does our world. By *being* the change we wish to see in the world—we change the world. Have you ever put together a jigsaw puzzle and not been able find the last piece? Suddenly, the last piece becomes the most important one. We are each an important piece of the cosmic puzzle. Our job is to make sure that our very important piece is added to the great mosaic.

While the First Principle implores us to detach from particular outcomes, the Second Principle reminds us that because everything matters, each step in pursuit of a goal is just as important as reaching the finish line.

---

*Taken together the first two principles
become the embodiment of "it's not
about me, but it's up to me."*

Yes, it's all about you—being the best *you* that you're capable of mustering at the time. Doing the best you can, where you are, with what you have, *is* your best. You are the artist and your life is the canvas. You paint and create your experience one brush stroke at a time. By acting consciously and with the intent of putting love into every action, you align with the greater part of you and the Universe at large.

Everything you do *matters*.

CHOICES

There are hundreds of decision points daily. Do we work late, sit in front of the TV, spend time with the children, or go to the gym? We literally build our future with every choice we make in our *now*.

I received this delightful letter from a dear friend who had been contemplating the Second Principle. I love how it beautifully illustrates the impact of the choices we make and how those choices influence our experience.

> *Today I had a long list of things I HAD TO DO in the garden. My daughter dropped off my three-year-old grandchild, Molly. Well, believe me, it would have been a long day for me if I tried to force things to happen my way.*
>
> *I have lots of paths through my gardens. "Follow me,"*
> *Molly said as she went zigzagging on her path through*

my garden, sometimes walking on the tiny seedlings that are just now popping up. Follow Molly I did. I gave up my need to do things my way. Today Molly was my teacher.

She trotted off to the blueberry bushes and wanted to know where the blueberries were. She saw the blossoms on the bush but didn't quite get how those blossoms would become berries. She found a worm while I was digging and took him for a long walk through the garden. She tried to clean him off. "Isn't he so cute?" she said to me. "I love worms."

Molly rode in my wagon on top of the leaves heading for the compost pile. She rode on top of the dirt going back to the garden. She chased the "birdies." She fed the fish in the pond (even though they aren't supposed to eat much when the weather is cold).

At one point Molly climbed into my wagon and was talking to "Bob."

"Who is Bob?" I asked.

"See him. See him. He's right there." She pointed to a tiny bug crawling on the bottom of the wagon.

Molly watered those little baby flowers soldiering up, seeking sunshine. Some of the seedlings were drowned. Some got no water at all. Molly, however, was thoroughly soaked.

After a while Molly and I sat down at her little table and had a cup of herbal tea. Molly loves to have tea parties.

I am so pleased Molly ruled the day. I am so lucky I got to meet Bob the Bug. I don't know if the "wee wittle worm" survived Molly's attempts to get it clean, but that worm was more loved than most. The seedlings that were lost today will never be missed, because unlimited abundance rules in my garden. The wind chimes Molly hit with a stick were more musical today than ever. The sky was blue, the sun was warm, and the fish were over-indulged with food sticks. Our moments shared at our tea party were a precious opportunity for me to realize how much EVERYTHING MATTERS.

There are no small things. I think in order to be in touch with the truth that everything matters, I must live in the moment. Not once all day did I have any regrets. I learned life, like my garden, has many paths. Joy happens in the moment." [2]

Our choices matter—each and every one. Our conscious awareness of this truth empowers us to make those choices that best contribute to our well-being.

POSITIVE FOCUS

"It's not what happens to you that determines how you feel but how you react to it." This has long been one of my favorite truisms. Contrary to popular belief, our happiness is not dependent upon what happens to us, for we can create happy moments by *choosing* them. In almost every situation, we have the opportunity to focus on what is positive and working in our lives—or on what is not. Both are valid realities, but here is the million-dollar question: which one makes you feel better when you focus on it?

Keeping a positive focus isn't a denial of problems that need to be addressed, nor is it being blindly optimistic. Difficulties can be addressed without dwelling on them. By turning our attention to what's working in our lives rather than focusing on what's not, we give happiness an opportunity to sprout.

When we focus on the negative and on what's *not* working in our lives, it often shows up in our communication as complaining. This is incredibly disempowering because the complaint is almost always about something we're powerless to change. The complaining, in turn, only adds to our existing feelings of powerlessness.

So how does one become a more positive person? It's not hard but it does take time—and conscious effort. Rerouting a mental habit can be at least as difficult as changing a physical one. A key fundamental of making any kind of change in behavior is *replacing the old behavior with a new one*, one small step at a time.

Each time you choose to focus on what is positive in your life, you create a replacement for your negative focus. The more you do it, the easier it becomes because you're rewarded by feeling better mentally and physically. By noticing what's going right in your life, what you're grateful for, and noting your successes, your brain signals your body that everything is okay and your stress levels plummet. In turn, this positive feedback loop increases your sense of well-being and provides the motivation to continue the new behavior.

---

*Our energy flows where
our attention goes.*

What you choose to focus on either adds to your sense of well-being or takes away from it. Choosing to be happy regardless of what's happening around you weans you from the belief that others are responsible for your happiness. It frees you from the belief that things need to happen a certain way or that people need to be doing a certain thing for you to be happy. By practicing feeling good, you train yourself to be happy.

Reflection

➢ Think for a moment of what you are grateful for in your life and notice how it changes the way you feel.

➢ Imagine how your day would be different if you chose to focus on what was going right in your life.

CONSCIOUS COMMUNICATION

We are constantly communicating both verbally and nonverbally in every aspect of our lives. It's vital to pay attention to how effectively we do it. Good communication is a conscious activity.

Some people get annoyed by the *conscious* part. I've heard people say things like, "I shouldn't have to think so much about what I'm going to say before I say it." Or better yet, "When I love someone I shouldn't have to censor everything I'm going to say."

Sometimes we give ourselves a pass and feel entitled to communicate from a defensive and reactive place. Loving communication is hardest when others are behaving poorly or pushing one of our "buttons." Although others are often unaware the button is even there, we may assume the worst of others and believe they *meant* to hurt or irritate us. Feeling emotionally stung, we see their actions as a sign of disrespect or disregard for our welfare and can feel justified in striking back.

Behaving badly will inevitably make you feel bad. If you believe you're being treated poorly, instead of responding in kind, it can be very helpful to look at your possible contribution to the interaction. Do you have a history of allowing the other person's poor behavior to slide without addressing the footprints he or she has been leaving on your back? Have you set clear boundaries and spoken up when those boundaries have been crossed?

Although we can't control others, people will often modify their behaviors to accommodate us if we give feedback in a constructive and respectful way. Communicating as clearly and as lovingly as we can definitely takes effort—but it returns to us in spades.

One way to improve your communication is to review your day and recall any communication challenges you faced. Did you act with love or did you react with anger? At the end of the day, pat yourself on the back for those times when you chose the right action and seek to learn from those times when you did not.

Reflection
> Think of a recent interaction that went poorly. How can you make a better choice in a similar circumstance the next time?

> What words could you use to function at your best in this situation?

APOLOGIES

One of the most healing acts on the planet is a sincere apology. Apologies matter because they are a way of saying "I'm very sorry I hurt you."

I grew up believing only wrongdoing warrants an apology, so I felt justified not giving one when there was no ill will intended on my part. If forced to apologize out of pressure or guilt, what typically resulted was half-hearted: "I'm really sorry you got so upset when you thought I was ignoring you." Unsaid, but clearly implied, was "I'm sorry you're so sensitive and I hope you'll get over your stuff."

Using wrongdoing as the only criterion for offering an apology falls far short of what is needed. That criterion must expand to include not only wrongdoing, but also any words or actions that *inadvertently* create pain in another. This casts a much broader net for apology-giving.

As an illustration of this, imagine that Jim tells a sexually laced joke to a group of ten people at a party. Nine of them think it's very funny and laugh uproariously, suggesting his joke was a hit. However, he notices that Sarah does not.

Later, as he leaves the room to refill his glass, he sees her sitting alone and notices her red, puffy eyes. He approaches her to ask if she's okay; she tells him the joke was hurtful because it reminded her of sexual abuse she had experienced as a child.

Here are my questions: Does Jim owe Sarah an apology even though others in the group were not offended? Is her reaction simply *her* issue? Did he really do anything wrong?

I can tell you my answer now is very different from what it would have been a few years ago: we are responsible *whenever* we bring pain to others, even if we're just accidentally tripping over their personal land mines. It isn't the tripping that's wrong. What's wrong is not cleaning up the mess we've unintention- ally made. Our good intentions gone awry don't excuse us from doing the best we can to make things whole again. By making it a practice to apologize whenever our words or actions have triggered pain in another, we sidestep the whole issue of making an apology dependent upon whether or not we think we did something wrong.

A genuine apology expresses regret for the pain caused and comes with a promise not to offend the person in the same way again. Using my example of the sexually laced joke, it might sound like this: "I'm so sorry for hurting you by telling an insensitive joke. It certainly was not my intention to hurt you and I'll do my best to use better discernment in the future. Is there anything I can do to make this right?"

The Second Principle reminds us to be more conscious of our communication and to use the healing power of apology when we make a misstep.

GETTING BACK UP

Did you know a flea can jump eight to ten inches high and more than a foot horizontally? That's more than 350 times its body length. In human terms it's like jumping the length of a football field!

However, it isn't difficult to impair the jumping ability of a flea. In an experiment that's been continually replicated, when fleas are put in a jar with a lid, they repeatedly try to jump out of the jar and of course, meet the resistance of the lid. Within a short time they display a very interesting phenomenon: they quickly learn to jump only as high as they could when the lid was on! In effect they learn to operate within their perceived limitations. Most notably, they do not recover from this change in perception.

Likewise, humans can fall prey to perceived limitations. When we stumble and fall short of our goals, it can be easy for us to focus on our personal shortcomings and convince ourselves we are powerless. This can be a slippery slope where we beat ourselves up and invite potential self-sabotage.

Consider Mark, who is trying to make healthy dietary changes. In front of the TV one evening, he gives in to a craving for ice cream and doesn't stop until he's eaten far more than he should. Overwhelmed by a sense of failure and convinced he is powerless to make consistent and lasting progress, he may be tempted to discard his dietary goals altogether. Rather than accepting his miscue and recommitting to his goals, Mark uses the experience as evidence that he can't succeed. Over time his self-sabotage results in weight gain and the negative cycle continues.

It doesn't have to be this way. Falling down is not a problem *as long as we get back up*. Fortunately we can choose to pick ourselves up off the floor and walk again. Each time this happens, we strengthen a neural pathway in the brain that says "I can." We get stronger when we learn from a mistake and refuse to be defeated by it. Rather than indulging in the fear that would disempower us, we become more trustful of our ability to weather life's challenges.

We are all on an evolutionary journey, both individually and collectively. It's a journey of discovery where we often learn what works by finding out what doesn't. To grow and evolve requires making mistakes. It can be very tempting for the wiser persons we are now to look back with self-condescension and judgment about choices we've made in the past. Yet most of the time we were doing our best *at that stage of our evolution*, and for that reason, it's important to forgive ourselves.

Getting back up is one of the most positive gifts we can ever give ourselves or another person. By accepting our imperfection and moving forward with more wisdom than we had before our stumble, we *are* functioning at our best. Mistakes made are seldom tragic, but a fear of making mistakes can result in a life that is.

SETTING BOUNDARIES

One of the most important ways we take care of ourselves is by setting appropriate boundaries. Although we all share a common connection, we still function with individual needs, wants, and desires. That reality makes setting personal boundaries a very necessary part of life.

"No, thank you, I'd rather not do that."

"Yes, you can give me a hug."

"You can stay with me for one week but no longer."

"Yes, I'm willing to help you brainstorm, but I don't want to see the project through to completion."

"I'm very sorry but I can't lend you the money you're asking for."

"Thanks for asking me but I'll need to take a rain check this time."

Setting boundaries is crucial to functioning well in this world. Every request that someone makes of us comes with the need for discernment about how much we are willing to give and what we are comfortable giving. Whether it be from love or from a sense of obligation, when we give so much that we hurt ourselves, it is *not* the most loving action.

Self-first is not the same as self-ish.

If a tree is to bear fruit and continue to do so, the roots of that tree must receive water. There is no selfishness in that action, for continuing to bear fruit depends upon it. Likewise, choosing what keeps you healthy and balanced is imperative if you are to extend love to others.

Flight attendants always instruct adult passengers to put oxygen masks on themselves before they put them on their children in the case of an airplane emergency. This is a good example of self-first and a reminder that we will be unable to help others unless we first help ourselves.

Selfish is thinking *only of you*—it's all about you. Self-first is taking responsibility for *taking good care of you*. That's a very big difference. Choose wisely and when in doubt—choose you. As the only person you have control over in this life, your well-being depends on it.

HONORING YOUR PHYSICAL BODY

We live in a physical universe and our bodies are the vehicles through which we experience everything around us. A body that is functioning well is crucial for brain health, emotional balance, physical locomotion, and the millions of internal processes that generally work incredibly well if we give our body what it needs.

The fuel you give your body (food), the movement you provide (exercise), and the rest you make available (sleep) each have a great impact on its health. When you don't give your body what it needs with proper maintenance, it eventually requires *high* maintenance. As Edward Stanley, the 3rd Earl of Derby said, "Those who think they have not time for bodily exercise will sooner or later have to find time for illness."[3]

Taking care of your physical needs makes it easier to be at your best. When you're in pain or sick, it's much harder to think well, love well, and have a positive attitude. When you neglect your body by not making its care a priority or when you take your health for granted, you're living on borrowed time for your quality of life will eventually diminish and your body will demand care. Doctor visits, side effects from drugs, chronic pain, and mounting physical limitations can increasingly come to dominate your time and focus as you nurse an unhealthy body.

Of course there are many who live with physical circumstances beyond their control, such as enduring chronic pain, that create an ongoing physical challenge in their lives. Yet regardless of the level of difficulties and physical challenges each of us face, we are responsible for working with our bodies as best we can.

Working to improve your diet, to find exercise that your body will tolerate, and to get deep and regular sleep goes a long way toward helping your body be at its best so you can be at yours!

SECOND PRINCIPLE AFFIRMATION

Everything Matters

Every thought I think, every word I speak, and everything I do matters. I seek to make good choices and to be guided by the power of love in every instance.

I claim my ability to respond with love rather than with fearful reaction. With a loving intent, I seek to be the clearest and most loving communicator I can be and when I am not, I will offer an apology.

I acknowledge the ripple effect of my actions and strive for impeccability in all my affairs. Right action strengthens not only me, but others as well.

I release my focus on that which is negative in my life and the lives of others. I choose to see what is working and to amplify it.

I ask for wisdom in establishing healthy boundaries for myself and for clear communication of them to others.

I choose to assume the best of others when I'm confused by their actions or troubled by their behavior. I release them from my judgment and I walk with a forgiving heart, for I recognize we are all on a journey of learning.

I seek to do the best I can—where I am—with what I have this day. I ask that the fullest potential in me be activated in all I do.

THE THIRD PRINCIPLE

Greater Is That Which Is within Me

For thousands of years we have recognized our spiritual existence—that which is greater than our physical world and our human selves. Virtually every culture has a creation story that recognizes we are products of something much larger than ourselves. We have expressed that recognition in religion, ritual, and philosophy by many names: God, Source, Allah, Brahman, Divine Intelligence, Universe, I AM, and numerous others.

What has not been realized and acknowledged as often is that *we are each a part of that originating Source*—we are spiritual beings having a human experience. The British novelist C.S. Lewis stated it more bluntly when he said, "You don't have a soul. You are a soul. You have a body."

The recognition of our greater self is not easy in a physical world. From the moment we are born, our focus is on physical survival. As infants we quickly learn that to survive we need food, comfort, and bodily care from a caretaker. Our senses constantly confirm that everything real is *physical*.

Over time and through our experience,
it becomes apparent and even
unquestionable
that all the riches to be had and all of our
worth in the world lie outside of us.
Lost in the game of life, we are fully human.

By the time we reach adulthood, the physical world has beckoned us in a million ways to give it our primary focus. We can easily become captive to it—and we often do. We become obsessed with money, with accumulation, with having the perfect relationship, with our physical appearance, with having the latest electronic gadgets. Incessant advertising tells us to put our time and money in those things outside of us with the promise they will bring us happiness and give us ever-greater physical and emotional security.

But seeking fulfillment in the world outside ourselves often results in addictions, unhealthy dependencies, and life-wrecking detours. A lifetime can be spent trying to find happiness and security where it doesn't exist. It's like the acorn looking outside itself for the oak tree. That which we seek is within us.

Eventually, after an accumulation of painful disappointments, most of us reach a point where we realize physical security is an illusion. As we grow older, it becomes clear that everything physical is in a constant process of deterioration. None of it is permanent—not our bodies or our brains, not our houses or our bank accounts. The world we learn to depend on for our security fails us because it must.

Those who choose monastic life as a spiritual pathway often do so because it eliminates many potential sources of worldly distraction. Monastic life provides a regimented structure, seclusion from the outside world, a de-emphasis of sexuality—all designed to take the focus off of one's humanity so the spiritual aspect of one's life can be nurtured. However, this lifestyle is clearly not the answer for most of the world.

Organized religions attempt to address our spiritual nature by providing a paradigm for understanding who we are and our purpose in the world. At their best, they seek to teach us how to be the highest expression of love in this world. At their worst, they disempower us by using fear as a motivator rather than teaching that the divine spark resides in us all and can be expressed as love.

In my case, as a young boy, my religion acknowledged I was created in the "image and likeness of God," but went to great lengths, in sermon after sermon, to emphasize that I was a lowly human whose purpose it was to become spiritual enough to gain access to a wonderful afterlife. I learned God surely existed—but not in humans and surely not in me.

When I ask my clients about their spiritual beliefs and what they see as their purpose in life, they rarely have coherent answers. Even those who are actively practicing their religion often stumble through their responses, for their beliefs have not translated into a working spirituality that is woven into their everyday lives.

The Third Principle is a statement that our true power lies in the *recognition* and *connection* with that which is greater within us—our greater self. And the highest expression of our greater self is in the form of energy we call *love*. It's a lesson every spiritual master has repeatedly taught us.

You are a spiritual being having a human experience. By claiming your spiritual connection and seeking to nurture it, you come to align your thoughts, words, and behaviors with your greater self—with love.

Greater is that which is within you than that which is in the world.

THAT WHICH IS GREATER

When electricity moves through a light bulb, it lights up the entire room. Even though the electricity is unseen, we don't question its existence because we experience its effects: we see the light it creates.

In a similar fashion, each of us is designed to express our non-physical self—our greater self—through our human experience. Those who do so exude an energy that is attractive and palpable, leaving us to wonder why they're different and how they've captured this radiant energy. Glowing with positivity, they seem genuinely happy—because they are. Unbound by a purely physical definition of themselves, they radiate *wholeness* because their human self is in alignment with their spiritual self . They are love expressed.

We've all had wonderful moments that have moved us beyond the boundaries of everyday experience, connecting us with the divine love within. It happens when gazing into a lover's eyes, when looking at a baby who is giggling with delight, or when coming upon a field full of bright, white daisies. Imagine being able to expand those moments by consciously and consistently connecting with your greater self. There are some excellent tools for doing so in the latter part of this book.

Each of us is born with our own particular set of gifts and talents. Like a unique snowflake, your potential is different from that of anyone else on the planet. As you develop your awareness and connection to the vast and untapped resource of your greater self, you gain access to a richness beyond this physical world for expressing your unique and best self.

But there is a catch: you must first acknowledge and claim your divine connection. Being unaware of your greater self is like having a million dollars in the bank but not knowing it's there. You remain poor despite the wealth that awaits you to claim it.

Reflection

➢ When do you acknowledge what is greater within you?

➢ How do you imagine your life would be different if you were more aware of your greater self?

BUILDING TRUST

Oceans cover nearly three quarters of our planet. They are magnificent and vast. Imagine dipping a thermos bottle into an ocean, filling it with water, and then capping it. There are two important points that I want you to wrap your brain around in this illustration. First, just because the water is no longer visible doesn't mean it doesn't exist. More importantly, even though the bottled water is but a tiny fragment of the large ocean, both are chemically identical—*all that is within the ocean is contained within the thermos!*

Likewise, our bodies are thermos bottles of sorts, containers for our greater self. That greater self is unseen, but it's there. Best of all, just as the bottled water is a part of the greater ocean, *so is our non-physical self a part of the greater Universe*. That's incredibly exciting because what that means is through our connection with the Universe, we have access to it for help and guidance. However, before we can trust that possibility to be true, we must first see evidence of its existence.

Trust is different from faith. Faith is a belief in something without having proof of its existence. Trust is based on results and is built one step at a time in any relationship, whether it's with a person or with the Universe.

Begin by asking the Universe to give you green lights when you need a smooth traffic flow; ask for a parking spot close to the store where you want to shop; ask to know what food is best for your body as you look at a menu. Make a note of how often what you ask for comes to you, or if you get the answer or clarity you were seeking. Partnering with the Universe is like having a private life coach who is constantly working for your highest good. It doesn't cost a penny but its value is priceless.

Try this

➢ During the next week, try asking the Universe for green lights in traffic, a parking place, or clarity regarding a question you'd like an answer to. Make a note of the results.

CONNECTING WITHIN

Dolphins are breathing mammals. They can stay underwater for about twenty minutes before coming to the surface for air. Submerged in water for most of their lives, dolphins must regularly connect with the life-giving resource of oxygen. Their sustenance requires that they partner with the world above them even though they largely function in the world below.

Humans are not so different. Immersed in our physical experiences and the outer world, our well-being suffers when we are not connecting with the richness within us. By choosing to connect to the highest within us, we step onto a superhighway that is our conduit to connecting with the Universe for needed help and guidance.

One of the easiest ways you can learn how to receive guidance from your greater self is by practicing the Five-Minute Meditation. I'll be teaching it to you later in this book. Connecting within is a uniquely individual process for each person and takes practice. Trust yourself and be patient. Over time, the process will become easier and more natural.

The Third Principle is a reminder of your spiritual nature and the importance of that connection. Connecting within is a conscious activity—you must choose it. Close your eyes and become the observer of your experience. Instead of doing, let yourself be. Allow yourself to gently shift into the peacefulness and fullness of your greater self.

STEPPING OFF THE MERRY-GO-ROUND

As a child I often went with my family to see movies at the local outdoor drive-in. It was common for families to go early, before the start of the film, so children could play on a playground in front of the large screen. There were swings, seesaws, and monkey bars, but my personal favorite was the merry-go-round. I was always the first one out of our car, sprinting at breakneck speed to climb aboard. It was brightly colored and had metal bars that riders would cling to for dear life as it turned at a dizzying speed. The significant force it created and the adrenaline rush from the threat of being hurled off the disc combined to make it a virtual child magnet.

When the spinning finally stopped, I was always extremely dizzy and a bit disoriented. Of course that was the fun of it! I also found I needed some time to physically rebalance before getting on again.

Life is often like a merry-go-round. Dizzy from the constant activity, sometimes all we can do is hang on for dear life. Fortunately we can learn to create balance even in the midst of busyness. One way to create internal balance is to give ourselves a few minutes each day to step away from the incessant activity in our lives to connect within.

Try this

➢ Set aside a few minutes each day to connect with your greater self.

➢ What is it like to experience that connection?

PRAYER

We have access to the Universe and can call on it for help. That process has most often been called "prayer." Through the power of thought and our connection with the Universe, we can direct helpful energy to a situation, another person, or ourselves.

Prayer is a very unique process for each individual. There is no one way to do it. As a visual person, I like to create visual representations as I pray so I can more effectively direct the energy of my prayer. I often picture a golden white light running from my heart to the person for whom I'm praying. If I'm praying for a group or an area of the world, I surround them or it with light as well. On the other hand, visualization needn't be a part of your prayer process, for it's your intent and focus that makes the difference.

But what happens when we use this process and what we're trying to manifest doesn't come about? What's going on when the change we pray for doesn't happen?

*We get what we want when what we want
is in alignment with what the
Universe wants for us.*[4]

When we pray for a particular outcome and it doesn't come to be, it's very tempting to conclude that our prayer wasn't answered. We tend to judge the power of prayer based on whether the results are in sync with what we are asking. To avoid placing ourselves in this conundrum there's a very useful disclaimer that can be placed at the end of a prayer: "I ask for this or

something better for the highest good of all." This is a powerful statement because it is a recognition that we see only a very
limited portion of the bigger picture and can't always know what
is for the highest good.

When what results is different from what we ask for, it
doesn't mean our prayer wasn't answered. It often means that
what resulted *was* for the highest good and what we asked for
was not. Our challenge then becomes acceptance.

When praying for another, it's helpful to remember we cannot
know what is best for another person. If my father has cancer, my
wishes and prayer might be for a total recovery. But what if in the
bigger picture an impending death is for his highest good? Most
of the time we have an idea of what we *think* the best outcome
would be in a given situation, but our own self-interests can easily color our perspectives. Have you ever had the experience of
praying for a certain outcome in your life and when you got it you
realized it was absolutely *not* for your highest good?

There is another explanation when our prayers for others
appear not to be answered: free will. Despite all the support
and loving energy we may send to a situation or to others, indi-
viduals still get to make their own choices. You might pray for
a loved one to change his habits so he can enjoy a good quality of life, yet he continues to spend long hours on the couch
eating potato chips. Free will reigns. Each of us creates our
life with the choices we make. Prayer will not control someone
else's actions.

Lastly, there is the issue of time. What we pray for often
does not manifest instantaneously. It can take time for things
to align before we see the positive effect of our prayer. Various
pieces of the puzzle may have to fall into place before a prayer is

answered in a way we would recognize. The lag time can make it difficult to see the cause and effect that builds confidence in the power of prayer.

Prayer is a gift of love. It's a process that allows us to have a profoundly positive impact on ourselves, others, and the world. When we watch painful events on the news or see situations and people in distress, we have an opportunity to direct healing energy where it's needed with our thoughts. By doing so, we utilize the power of our connection with the Universe and become a much-needed part of the solution.

The Serenity Prayer is very common among twelve-step recovery groups:

> "Lord grant me the serenity to accept the things
> I cannot change, the courage to change the things
> I can, and the wisdom to know the difference."

There is a striking correlation between the first three principles and this prayer.

➢ The *serenity to accept the things I cannot change* is very much the focus of "nothing has to happen my way."

➢ *The courage to change the things I can* is an application of "everything matters."

➢ *And the wisdom to know the difference* is embodied by Principle Three, where the connection within provides the wisdom and discernment needed for right action.

THIRD PRINCIPLE AFFIRMATION

Greater Is That Which Is within Me

I begin this day with the recognition that my connection with my greater self is greater than anything outside of me.

I give myself the timeless experience of being in the precious now. Like a dolphin filling its lungs with life-giving oxygen as it comes to the surface, I will connect within for renewal during my day so I am centered and balanced.

I choose to honor my greater self by making time to align with it. I will step off the merry-go-round of constant activity so my perspective is clear and my choices are in alignment with right action.

As I go forth this day, I choose to see through the eyes of my greater self and ask for guidance. I commit to *seeing* what is needed and to *being* what is needed so I may be an expression of love and positive action in the world.

I will direct energy in the form of prayer to those people and situations that come into my awareness, letting go of my version of what I think would be the best outcome by sending healing and wholeness for the highest good of all.

I claim the power I have to express love and will joyfully look for those moments when I can express it.

THE FOURTH PRINCIPLE

Be the Miracle

Every moment offers us the opportunity to see miracles. Whether it's the incredible functions of our brains, the complex relationship between plants and the air they purify, or the marvel of childbirth—we are surrounded by the miracles of life. With carbon-based bodies made of the very elements that comprise our physical planet and the stars, we *are* a grand miracle.

Seeing miracles connects us to the magic of life and keeps us in a place of wonder. That's the space that comes so easily to children who have not yet been tarnished by so much busyness that they fail to notice. Maintaining that place of wonder is a miracle, for most of us don't. Yet it's always there for us.

---

*The key to seeing miracles
each day is to look for them.*

Miracles come to us as the delicious fullness of a favorite meal, the playful shenanigans of a young kitten, the sound of gurgling water as it runs over stones, the comfort of cozying up to read a book on a rainy day, and the smell of air after a summer rain. Beauty and wonder are everywhere on this planet.

We can fill ourselves with wonder by looking at the world through the fresh eyes of a child. Aging can be helpful in this regard. No longer feeling the invincibility and immortality of youth, we come to realize the fragility and temporal nature of our time on this planet. Death may yet be a very distant visitor, but its eventuality enters our awareness. It can profoundly change the way we see life, allowing the sense of wonder we had as children to return—this time through an adult brain.

That perspective is a gift, for with it we begin to treasure our present moments as the miracles they are. With a growing awareness of our mortality, meals are savored, sunrises are embraced, and grandchildren are adored.

In addition to becoming aware of the miracles that surround us, we can actively *be* the miracle. In the physical world, a tsunami can be created by a single shift in the earth's tectonic plates. A single act of love can likewise be transformative. History is replete with examples of those who have achieved greatness and who in turn credit something done by a parent, a teacher, a stranger, or a friend that served as a catalyst to propel them to that level of high functioning. The ripple effects of our positive actions are often not as easy to see as a tsunami, but they are no less powerful.

Our loving actions create miracles. This concept can seem foreign if we don't believe that acts of love truly do create extraordinary and positive outcomes. By making it a practice to *be* what is needed rather than focusing on what *we* need, we become a living expression of love and a positive agent for change in the world.

> **Reflection**
> ➢ When was the last time you witnessed a miracle?
> ➢ Can you recognize a miracle that has happened today?

RESPECT AND RECOGNITION

Every human desires two things: respect and recognition. Treating others with respect and giving them recognition can create miracles.

One day a friend of mine was called on to be a substitute teacher of an unruly class. From the moment she entered the classroom, several students gave her a hard time. They probably thought they could get away with misbehaving, knowing she would only be subbing for a day or two. After several disruptions, my friend did a very interesting thing. Noticing there were no windows in the room, she calmly walked over to the light switch and turned off the lights—not out of anger or for retribution, but for effect. It was pitch black.

What she did next was something the students could never have imagined in their wildest dreams. In a tender voice she said, "You may not know this, but you are incredible. You are smart and you are beautiful. I am so privileged to be with you today and am excited about our time together. This is going to be a great day."

When she turned the lights back on, you could have heard a pin drop. These students were literally transformed by her loving recognition of them and the respect with which she addressed them. Rather than focusing on their current misbehavior—the smaller version of themselves—she helped them to recognize the greater part of themselves. Through the power of that one act where respect and recognition were freely given, she likely changed the lives of those students on that magical day.

This story is a beautiful example of how one person can be an instant miracle in the lives of others by seeing the best in them. Being generous with respect and recognition draws people to us like bears to honey. When clients tell me they have no friends in their lives, I ask them how frequently they hand out the gifts of respect and recognition to others. Far too often they are waiting with open arms to receive what they have not yet given.

When we haven't learned that giving respect is the best way to get it, we may resort to seeking it in other ways. This might show up as obtaining praise from a boss by being a workaholic, getting strokes from others by being a people pleaser, or feeling flattered by having an illicit affair.

In her book *Loving What Is*,[5] Byron Katie says she does not pray, but if she did her prayer would be: "God, spare me from the desire for love, approval, or appreciation. Amen." I love the wisdom behind that prayer because it recognizes that seeking love, approval, and appreciation is an upside-down strategy. Love comes to us when we *give* it.

ASSUMING THE BEST

One of the greatest lessons I have learned in life is that I can never know another person's intent. My past is littered with painful instances where I have misjudged others by assuming the worst of them. This is a huge source of conflict in many relationships and is regretful because the truth is very few people in the world are roaming about with ill intent. When we assume the worst of others, we are almost always grossly mistaken.

Consider the case where another driver swerves in front of your car with no turn signal, causing you to hit your brakes. With an overload of adrenaline racing through your system, what's your first assumption? Do you assume the driver is thinking only of himself and is therefore willing to risk your safety? Do you want to punish him for being such a terrible driver? In both of these instances, there is likely an assumption that the driver is not concerned for your safety.

I have occasionally been that driver and have accidentally cut people off in traffic. Yet, I am not a terrible driver, nor do I ever intend to create a dangerous situation. Sometimes I've failed to see someone in my blind spot. At other times I've been deep in thought and not as attentive to those around me as I should have been. Once I had just heard some unwelcome news about my mother's health and my focus was definitely compromised.

These were factors unknown to the drivers around me. How could anyone have possibly known my intent or what I was dealing with? The answer, of course, is they could not. When we assume the worst of others, we create a negative narrative in our head that is rarely true.

Visualize this scenario: You're standing in a wall-to-wall crowd of people at a concert. You abhor crowds but your love for the band overrides your uneasiness. Suddenly you feel a jab below your right shoulder blade. It startles you but you assume it was an accidental bump. It happens again—this time with even more force. Your face flushes with anger as your mind races with thoughts of how inconsiderate other people can be. As you whirl around, ready to burn a hole in the person who seems oblivious to the pain being inflicted upon you, you come eye to eye with a person wearing a full arm cast in a sling. What do you think now? Do your feelings change?

It's likely they do for something very powerful has happened. What changed was the story you told yourself. Perhaps a wave of compassion washed over you as your righteous anger yielded to nonjudgment. Although the pain you experienced was real, your judgment of it changed as you realized your assumption of the other person's intent was in error.

Negative thoughts give rise to negative reactions. It doesn't feel good to get angry by thinking the worst of others. Assuming the best of others is a great example of being the miracle because it keeps you from creating unneeded drama and places others in the best light possible until there is evidence to the contrary. Best of all, you'll usually be right when you assume the best!

CHOOSING LOVE

Choosing to love has huge payoffs: peace, happiness, and well-being. These are sweet fruits that money can't buy. Is it harder to choose love than not to? Sometimes it is. But most of the time choosing otherwise is just a bad habit that can almost always be replaced by a healthier one.

I recently stopped at a traffic light next to a very dilapidated vehicle. Its engine was struggling mightily as it idled. The rear window was gone, covered with plastic held in place by gray and peeling duct tape. The back bumper dangled perilously. On the passenger side a woman, clearly weathered by life, smoked a cigarette that hung limply from her fingers. The driver was unkempt and unshaven.

As I gazed at these two people, I found myself constructing a negative narrative. Judgments and labels began to flood my mind and work their way into the story I was composing. I wondered what decisions they had made that put them in their current situation. How could they have let their lives, choice by choice, come to this undesirable place?

Suddenly an internal switch was flipped. Although I had composed a similar narrative many other times in my life, this time it wasn't okay. As I caught myself putting this couple in a negative box with my personal assessment, I realized I had another choice in front of me—a better one. I could spend my time in judgment and conjecture regarding the state of their lives, or I could be a positive force by directing energy to help.

This time I chose the latter. I claimed my connection with the Universe and surrounded them with wholeness and healing. I visualized them receiving clarity and discernment to help them make the right choices in their lives. Finally, I asked the Universe to bring this couple prosperity and to protect them in all situations in their lives.

Was it difficult? It wasn't. It took not an ounce more mental effort to choose a loving action than it did to create my negative story about this couple. What amazed me was how much it positively changed *my* experience.

Very grateful for the awareness of that day, I realized how many opportunities there are to turn judgmental thoughts into loving ones; to direct loving energy rather than to ignore; and to make a difference in the world, even in the most mundane of circumstances. It showed me love is always an option and when I give it, it comes back to me and changes me for the better.

GRATITUDE

Gratitude is the recognition of the gifts in our lives. When we acknowledge what is working in our lives, the beauty that surrounds us, the abundance we have, and our connection with the Universe, we are expressing gratitude.

Cultivating gratitude is so integral to our well-being that I often ask clients to write down five gratitudes a day for at least three weeks. Many initially have difficulty with this because they think much too broadly. They quickly exhaust their gratitudes by listing their health, their job, their home, etc.

What I want them to do instead is to move from listing broad categories to identifying *specific* experiences they are grateful for each day. This might include their car starting when the key is turned, getting much-needed rain, having hot coffee to start the day, enjoying the luxury of air conditioning while driving to work, completing a task in a timely way, or being the recipient of a friend's warm smile.

Gratitude comes easiest for things we appreciate, such as a sumptuous dinner, a spectacular sunset, or beautiful, pink cherry blossoms. When the event is unwanted—a car breaking down, a disagreement with a partner, or being fired from a job—seeing the silver lining and being grateful can be a challenge.

Dealing with the immediacy of a loss or a stressful event is not the only challenge, for the greater task is maintaining a positive perspective and being open to new possibilities for something equally wonderful to enter our lives. Healing occurs when we eventually reach the place where we are grateful for the unwanted event because we can recognize the gifts that have come from it.

Cultivating gratitude opens your eyes to the many gifts that fill your day that might otherwise go unnoticed. Teaching yourself to notice the positive aspects that make up your day helps you stop sweating the small stuff. Gratitude rocks.

Reflection

➢   Think of five things you are grateful for in your life.

➢   How does thinking about these gratitudes make you feel?

LOVE IS A MIRACLE MAKER

Love is powerful. Loving words and actions leave indelible footprints on our hearts, touching our lives in empowering ways. Think back to a time in your life when someone touched your heart with an act of love. Simply recalling it likely rekindles the feelings you had at the time. That's the power and the miracle of love.

We all want love—we crave it, we long for it, we even dream about it. Why then, is it so hard to love? Why is it so difficult to be, what at our very core we already are?

One reason it's hard is because we don't believe love will protect us. We don't trust it to work for us nor do we see it as something powerful in our lives. As a result we often buy multiple shares of stock in Fear, Inc., investing our precious resources of time and energy in pursuits and behaviors that can never give us the true richness we seek.

If love is so powerful, and it certainly is, then how do we bring that miracle into our lives? There is a sure-fire solution: give it generously. But this suggestion flies in the face of human logic. Living in a physical world, we get tripped up because we are constantly confronted by what appears to be limited abundance. If you have four oranges and give me three, then you only have one left. How can it possibly help to give away what you're trying to get?

The answer, of course, is that love is not bound by the laws of the physical world. Love is synergistic and infinitely abundant. The more we give, the more we get.

There's a story that's been retold many times about Milton Erickson, a famous psychiatrist who was very successful at treating people with difficult mental disorders. This story touches me deeply because it illustrates the powerful influence that giving love has upon both the giver and the receiver:

> *A favorite aunt of one of Erickson's colleagues was living in Milwaukee and had become quite seriously depressed. When Erickson gave a lecture there, the col-*

league asked him to visit the aunt and see if he could help her. The woman had inherited a fortune and lived in the family mansion. But she lived all alone, never having married, and by then had lost most of her close relatives. She was in her sixties and had medical problems that restricted her to a wheelchair, severely curtailing her social activities. She had begun to hint to her nephew that she was thinking of suicide.

The great doctor agreed to make just one visit to the house. Dr. Erickson was surprised by what he saw. The lady lived in squalor beyond anything he had ever experienced. All the curtains were closed, making the house a depressing place indeed. As he made a tour of the house, he noticed one wilting African violet. At the end of the tour, he said, "I can tell you love flowers." The lady agreed that she did.

At the end of their time together, Dr. Erickson advised the woman to grow the flowers she loved so much, and to send these flowers to each person she found in the local paper who had given birth, was celebrating a wedding, or was grieving a death. Although it seemed like a very odd request to her, the lady reluctantly agreed and began to watch the paper for new births, weddings, and deaths.

News spread quickly throughout the city about the mysterious woman who was sending people African violets. She quickly discovered others were profoundly touched that someone they didn't know would take the time to acknowledge them in their pain or their joy. This lady, who had been markedly depressed, created a sense of purpose in her life through a relatively simple act that created a network of love with those whose lives she touched. She was truly transformed through the gratitude and appreciation expressed by the recipients of her loving actions.

Upon her death there was a feature article with a large headline that read "African Violet Queen of Milwaukee Dies, Mourned by Thousands." The article detailed the life of this incredibly caring woman who had become famous for her trademark flowers and her charitable work with people in the community during the ten years preceding her death. Needless to say, her depression had been transformed by the power of loving action. One simple change in behavior—giving what she needed to receive—had a powerful impact on her and on the world.[6]

This remarkable story shows the power we have to transform lives through love. We can choose to make someone's day better and brighter in many ways. Giving a compliment, lending a helping hand, sending an anonymous gift, writing a thank-you note, attentively listening—all are powerful gifts that change the lives of those with whom we come into contact.

---

*It is expressing our love
that creates miracles.*

Very often those who tend to be negative and difficult to deal with have poor self-images. When we respond in a way that allows them to think the best of themselves, we give them a gift they are unable to give themselves. Because we all yearn for love, it's a rare character who will not respond to it by being warmer and more congenial. No, it doesn't happen all the time, but in most situations we train people how to treat us and we truly get back what we give.

Love is like a savings account with compound interest: the more we deposit, the larger the return on that investment. We have the opportunity in every moment to choose love or not and each moment awaits the potential miracle of our making that choice. Making someone's day better and brighter fills us up on the inside. It's a powerful cure for depression and the belief that what we do doesn't really matter.

Love is the biggest miracle maker of all. By assuming the best of others, being respectful, and expressing gratitude for the positive actions of others, we make it much more likely they will respond in kind.

Be the miracle!

FOURTH PRINCIPLE AFFIRMATION

Be the Miracle

I open myself to the wonder of this day and to seeing the miracles that surround me.

I am a living miracle of love. I choose to function today as love by being what is needed.

As I go through this day, I will focus on what is working and be filled with gratitude for the abundance in my life.

I choose to be a miracle today by functioning at my highest in every situation.

I commit to giving others recognition and being respectful in all my communications.

I choose to see others today through fresh eyes. I release any former judgments that keep me from experiencing them as they are today.

I choose happiness by focusing on what is working in my life and by seeing the miracles that surround me.

If I fall short today, I will embrace my effort rather than judging the stumble.

I choose to be a living example of doing the best I can, wherever I am, with what I have.

THE FIFTH PRINCIPLE

I Surrender My Humanness

"A human being is part of the whole, called by us 'Universe,' limited in time and space. A human experiences thoughts and feelings as something separated from the rest—a kind of optical delusion of consciousness. This delusion is a prison, restricting us to our personal desires and to affection for a few persons close to us. Our task must be to free ourselves from our prison by widening our circle of compassion to embrace all humanity and the whole of nature in its beauty."

—*Albert Einstein*[7]

The Third Principle is the recognition of the divine in you as your greater self. The Fourth Principle implores that you be the miracle by being a loving and positive force in the world. The Fifth Principle goes one step further. "I surrender my humanness" is not only a recognition of your greater self but a statement of your intent to allow it to *guide your life*. With that decision you open the door to functioning in loving wholeness, where your spiritual self expresses itself through your human one.

We are designed to function
in loving wholeness.

Surrendering your humanness may sound like a sacrifice, but it's not. Exchanging a life perspective fraught with insecurity, frailty, confusion, and fear for a partnership with the Universe based on wisdom, right choice, and love is a welcomed gift. This conscious and chosen surrender brings about a remarkable transformation—one that Jesus, Krishna, Buddha, Confucius, and every spiritual master on this planet has said we are capable of and has asked us to make.

Those who function in wholeness are recognizable in numerous ways. The traits and behaviors they embody include:

> ➤ Living in the moment, trusting they have what they need in each moment.

> ➤ Knowing they create their internal experiences and taking responsibility for doing so.

> ➤ Loving themselves.

> ➤ Forgiving themselves and others.

> ➤ Freeing themselves from the prison of comparative judgment.

> ➤ Taking responsibility for clear and loving communication.

> ➤ Adapting well to change.

> ➤ Releasing expectations.

> ➤ Displaying a deep sense of gratitude for the many gifts in their lives.

➢ Honoring their physical bodies by eating well, exercising, and getting proper rest.

➢ Accepting their bodies and allowing them joyful expression through healthy sexuality and sensuality.

➢ Finding meaning and miracles in the mundane.

➢ Laughing at themselves and with others.

➢ Accepting the moment without judging that it should be different than it is.

We've all had moments when we've functioned as our best and most loving selves. By consciously working to surrender our humanness, we *increase* and *extend* those moments so joyful living becomes a more frequent companion. As we work to release our tendency to focus solely on our security needs, it becomes easier to align with what we truly are: beings of love.

BEING THE PERSON YOU WANT TO SEE IN THE WORLD

It's so easy for us to want *others* to be more responsible, loving, and trustworthy. But the reality is that we can only control ourselves. Rather than bemoaning the state of the world and the people in it, we can seek to become the kind of person we want to see in the world. As Mahatma Gandhi so eloquently said, we must become the change we want to see. Unfortunately, we can't flip a switch to quickly bring that about. Transformation happens by consistently taking one tiny step at a time.

Imagine starting each day with the goal of being the person you want to see in the world, taking note of each time your greater self wins out over your human one. Perhaps you only have one of those moments the first day. But if you can choose one moment, you can choose three the next day. And if you can choose three, you can choose six.

Others will notice. Step by step and with a consistent focus, you can create a life you love—a life *of* love. We truly do change the world by changing ourselves, and we only change ourselves with love.

SERVICE

Volunteering is a marvelous doorway to the surrender of our humanness. It allows us to move our focus beyond ourselves by giving our time to something or someone without an expectation of receiving anything in return.

I often suggest volunteering to my clients who report symptoms of boredom, depression, or lack of purpose in their lives. However, because they already feel depleted of energy with nothing left in their emotional tanks, their reactions are often less than enthusiastic. Overburdened by everyday obligations such as working and parenting, they balk at giving more of themselves. In many cases they have become so focused on their own needs that it's difficult for them to believe that giving to others could be a realistic antidote. Unaware that giving love is the doorway to receiving it, they often retreat from the very thing that could renew their energy reserves.

Giving can also be anonymous. Sending money, mailing a "thank you" card, or paying for the person's order behind you at a fast food drive-through window are all powerful acts of love because the recipients are often deeply touched by the validation that someone cares enough to give without a need for recognition. It can help to restore their faith in humanity.

Giving when we are not obligated to do so is what makes volunteering and anonymous giving so special. It's one of the easiest ways of saying "yes" to love.

Reflection
➤ Consider giving your time to a project or cause that really matters to you and is close to your heart. Serving in a way that utilizes your particular talents can make it a fun and rewarding process.

YOUR HIGHEST AND BEST

> *"The day will come when, after harnessing space, the winds, the tides and gravitation, we shall harness for God the energies of love. And on that day, for the second time in the history of the world, we shall have discovered fire."*
> —*Pierre Teilhard de Chardin*[8]

We resist the thought that we are powerful because it frightens us. We are uncomfortable with the responsibility that comes with being living representations of loving energy on earth. We are more comfortable when we make ourselves smaller, pointing to our human imperfections as evidence we are anything *but* that greater representation.

The good news is perfection is not a requirement on planet earth. In fact, trying to be perfect only gets in the way. It's about consciously choosing to do the best we can. But how do we know if we're doing that?

Here are several questions you can ask yourself to help in your effort to live your best:

> What is the most loving thing to do in this situation?
> What is the best right action?
> What is for the greatest good?
> What will bring healing to this situation?

Each time you choose to function in alignment with your greater self, you function *as* your greater self. As you experience the successes this brings, it fuels your motivation and gives you confidence to do it more often. Over time your acts of love become more automatic, and like a small stone sending ripples across a large lake, touch the world in beneficial ways.

FORGIVENESS

We often resist the very notion of forgiveness. Hanging on to a resentment can easily be justified when we feel our forgiveness of another isn't warranted. If we believe that forgiveness means letting the perpetrator off the hook and condoning their behavior, we may tenaciously cling to our sense of justifiable outrage.

Yet here is the cruel irony: as long as we justify our anger and keep the memory alive by reliving it and retelling it to ourselves and others, *we* become the perpetrator of our continued pain. In many instances the original transgression was short-lived. When we keep the memory alive and vow never to forgive, we consistently breathe life into the original drama.

Forgiveness is often misunderstood. The purpose of forgiveness is not to absolve another of wrongdoing or to condone their hurtful behavior, Rather, it's a gift that brings *healing to the one who has been injured.*

When Jesus said, "Love your enemies," it wasn't meant as a directive to roll over and invite abuse. It was a prescription for releasing oneself from the cruelty of keeping a painful memory alive. Forgiveness brings welcome relief through releasing the ongoing judgment of another.

If we truly want justice for
the pain we have experienced,
then we must release it for it is
unjust that we continue to suffer.

If there is pain in your life because of another, you must release it before healing can take place. By grieving your pain and then releasing it as quickly as possible, you refuse to wear victimization as a badge of retribution and see it as the albatross around your neck that it is. You can and must turn away the obsessive thoughts that so often take root when you are hurt. The person who hurt you may not deserve your good thoughts—but *you* do. Hanging on to your resentment of another can cost you months or years of wasted time. There is no retribution in holding on to anger for you are the only one who continues to hurt.

Self-forgiveness is also needed. We all make some pretty dumb decisions at times. Who among us cannot look back with a reddened face at something we would never again repeat? Making peace with our personal choices in the past can sometimes be difficult.

A few years ago, a good friend shared a very useful tool that helped me learn to forgive myself. She told me to close my eyes and picture the person I was when I did what I now regretted. She then asked me to allow myself to feel compassion and to imagine myself putting my arms around that person, comforting him for not being wise enough at the time to make a better decision.

The effects were profound and healing. I was able to replace my critical judgment with much-needed compassion. Rather than continue my self-bludgeoning, I accepted what was. This powerful tool also enabled me to update my internal self-image by celebrating the wiser person I am now. I use this visualization whenever needed and strongly encourage you to try it too.

Reflection

➤ Who have you not forgiven?

➤ What would you need to do to release yourself from that continued pain?

UNITY CONSCIOUSNESS

Surrendering our humanness for the greater good is improbable without an awareness that we are all "one." The great Sufi poet Rumi spoke beautifully of our oneness.

> One went to the door of the Beloved and knocked.
> A voice asked, "Who is there?"
> He answered, "It is I."
> The voice said, "There is no room for Me and Thee."
> The door was shut.
> After a year of solitude and deprivation he
> returned and knocked.
> A voice from within asked, "Who is there?"
> The man said, "It is Thee."
> The door was opened for him.
>
> —Jelaluddin Rumi[9]

Although the recognition of our interconnectedness can be difficult given the countless forms of diversity on this planet, the explosion in technological advances in recent years has made a positive contribution to that growing recognition. The boundaries that once made people from other lands seem alien are now virtually irrelevant. As we discover the truth that we are all a part of something much larger, we are expanding our consciousness to a level never before experienced in human history.

As we awaken to our interconnectedness with each other and the planet, it becomes harder to sustain the perceptions of *us* and *them*. We're on a journey together, one that requires us to move beyond the chaos and strife to find a way of creating unity. When our hearts are centered in the recognition that we are all one, we understand that what we do for each other we are doing for ourselves as well.

Jesus spoke of such action: "Do unto others as you would have them do unto you" and "Whatever you do to the least of my brothers, that you do unto me." By recognizing that we are all a part of a greater whole, we claim the global village as family.

I am you—you are me—we are one.

FIFTH PRINCIPLE AFFIRMATION

I Surrender My Humanness

I choose to give what is needed rather than focusing solely on what I need.

I recognize and embrace the interconnectedness of all life.

I surrender my humanness to flow with that which is for the highest good in every situation I encounter today.

I surrender my humanness by releasing any fear surrounding money, my body, or my relationships.

I surrender to my greater self and welcome its guidance.

I free myself from continued pain by letting go of judgment and forgiving those who have hurt me.

I endeavor to be the person I want to see in the world by thinking, speaking, and acting with love as my guide.

A SUMMARY

The First Principle: *Nothing Has to Happen My Way*
This principle dispels the belief that our lives need to unfold in accordance with our personal desires for us to be happy. It directs us to give up all forms of controlling behavior and helps us to cultivate the fruits of *acceptance* and *detachment*.

The Second Principle: *Everything Matters*
We create our lives moment by moment through the choices we make. This principle asks us to be responsible and to make the best right choices consciously because everything we do matters. It offers the fruits of *right action* and *responsibility*.

The Third Principle: *Greater Is That Which Is within Me*
This principle is a recognition that we are more than our physical self. We are spiritual beings having a human experience. Through the recognition of our greater self, we can learn to access its wisdom and guidance to help us function at our best. The fruits of this principle are *inner connection* and *empowerment*.

The Fourth Principle: *Be the Miracle*

This principle asks us to be the change we seek in the world—to become the miracle. By looking for opportunities to express love, we transform those with whom we have contact. The fruits of this principle are *loving expression* and *positive function*.

The Fifth Principle: *I Surrender My Humanness*

The Fifth Principle is a statement of surrendering a focus on our human security needs to allow our spiritual self to express through our physical self. The fruits of this principle are *service* and *wholeness*.

The figure below is a visual illustration of the integration of our dual aspects as we work with the Five Principles.

Greater Self   Wholeness

Human Self

Principle 1 → Principle 2 → Principle 3 → Principle 4 → Principle 5

Now that you have familiarized yourself with the Five Principles, you can begin the process of working with them. In the pages ahead you'll find many useful tools to help you do so.

Let's get started!

INTEGRATING
THE PRINCIPLES

LIVING YOUR BEST

*A Powerful Program
for Personal Transformation*

*"No man ever steps in the same river twice, for it's
not the same river and he's not the same man."*
—*Heraclitus*[10]

Who you are now is *not* the person you were in your past. Not
a year ago, a month ago, or even yesterday. The truth is we are
constantly undergoing change as we adapt to an ever-changing
world.

One of the biggest obstacles to personal transformation is
that we often create fixed identities of who we think we are.
Justifications such as "that's just the way I am" bolster the belief
that positive change is outside our grasp. They also provide con-
venient excuses for not making positive changes.

Before starting this program, I want to encourage you to begin
with the intent of releasing old patterns and beliefs that no longer
serve you. Close your eyes, quiet yourself, and make a commitment to willingly surrender who you have been so you may choose
to become a greater version of you, happy and functioning at your
best. Do it right now.

Through the power of your intent and your thoughts, this sets into motion the creation process toward that which you desire. Lastly, ask the Universe to partner with you to give you the help you need to make your vision a reality.

Now let's make some positive and life-enhancing changes!

REPATTERNING YOUR BRAIN

You are a creator whether you want to be or not. You cannot *not* create. Your intent gives rise to your thoughts, your words, and your actions in a sequence of steps that are a part of every creation. Consciously using this process is vital to creating what you want to experience in the world.

THE CREATION PROCESS

Intent   Thoughts   Words   Actions

As an example of this process, let's imagine you want to create a small backyard garden. That is your *intent*. You begin to *think* about where the sunlight and soil will be best for it and what you will need to maintain it. You *talk* to others, read what others have written, and ask others for their input. Finally you reach the point where you *act* on your plans and voilá—you have created your garden.

Integrating the Five Principles occurs primarily at the level of *thought*. Once you make it your intent to integrate the principles and consistently focus on them with your thoughts, you'll find that your words and actions align with them.

Most people don't grasp the immense power their thoughts have to shape their life experiences. They relegate thinking to the silent voices in their heads—as *only* thoughts—but those thoughts create. For that reason it's very important to control which thoughts we allow to flow through our heads. They are a vital part of the creation process because our words and actions flow from them.

We are choosy about our cars,
our clothes, and how we like
our coffee—but often we are
not choosy about our thoughts.

As you work to integrate the Five Principles, you will literally be remapping your brain. Research has shown that when we consciously replace old thoughts with new ones, we create new neural pathways that result in physiological changes in our brains. The term for this phenomenon is *neural plasticity*, one of the most exciting discoveries in the field of human behavior.

In his book, *Buddha's Brain*,[11] Rick Hanson explains how changes in our thinking are reflected on a physiological level in our neural anatomy. Our neural pathways continually rearrange themselves throughout the course of our lives, allowing our brains and nervous systems to adapt to an endless number of different situations. This has huge implications because it means we can create new neural networks and override pre-existing ones. Over time, as new neural pathways are strengthened through conscious thought, it takes less and less effort to engage in the desired behavioral change. How's that for the power of thought? *We are changing our brains when we change our thoughts!*

But making those changes requires practice and consistency. We understand and accept that we have to practice physical skills such as playing the saxophone, singing, or sculpting to become skilled at them. We may not realize we also have to practice our thoughts to become skilled at thinking with a positive focus. Just as you wouldn't plant weeds in your vegetable garden, it's vital to make sure the thoughts you cultivate on a regular basis will bring about the harvest you want in your life.

There are no shortcuts. Choosing thoughts that align with the Five Principles changes your experience and the neural patterning in your brain. The more you focus on them, the faster they become *you*.

HELPFUL SUGGESTIONS

Here are some excellent ways to make the integration of the principles a conscious, daily practice.

- ➤ Start each day by focusing on a particular principle. State it aloud with a strong resolve to make it the lens through which you filter your experiences that day.

- ➤ Close your eyes and imagine the neural pathways in your brain being rewired so changes can be made easily and permanently.

- ➤ Use negative thoughts and emotions as opportunities to practice the particular principle you're working on to change your experience and make it more positive. For example, if you're working on the Fourth Principle, "Be the Miracle," and you feel grumpy, use your grumpiness as a reminder that you can choose a different perspective that brings you good feelings.

EXTERNAL REMINDERS

Awareness and consistent practice are essential. The more reminders you build into your life, the faster you'll progress. Here are a few suggestions to help you stay focused on the principles as you work with them.

- ➢ For a visual reminder, consider tying a thin, colored ribbon or string around your wrist to represent the First Principle. Tell yourself that every time you see it you'll think about that specific principle and reflect on how you're putting it into practice. As you work with each principle in turn, add a different color. The ribbons can be great conversation starters when people ask why you are wearing them.

- ➢ Put a printed copy of the Five Principles on your dashboard, on your vanity, or on your refrigerator. Put it where you will see it every day to keep it in the forefront of your awareness.

- ➢ For an auditory reminder, consider setting your watch or cell phone to signal you every couple of hours or at whatever interval works best for you. Use the reminder to focus briefly on the principle you're working with at the time.

- ➢ You can also train yourself to use times of inactivity as reminders to reflect upon the principles. This might include time spent waiting at stoplights, watching television commercials, and waiting in lines.

JOURNALING

Another powerful tool for transformation is journaling. I've worked with enough people over the years to know that some would rather sift through sawdust than journal their experiences. Journaling is helpful for a number of reasons:

> ➤ It encourages you to think through and process your ongoing experiences.

> ➤ It provides a consistent focus that makes adherence to the program an easier process.

> ➤ It creates an easy way to track your progress. This builds confidence and as trust because you can clearly see the changes you make over time.

Consider buying an inexpensive journal to use solely for your work with the principles. As many have discovered, once you get in the flow of journaling, you'll find yourself looking forward to it.

WORKING WITH THE PROGRAM

It would be wonderful if we could swing like Tarzan, sailing across a vast divide and undergoing a magnificent personal transformation in one fell swoop. But in reality change happens one step at a time, and the small steps we take in our moment-to-moment present are the ticket to lasting change.

There's a longstanding maxim in the personal growth field that it takes twenty-one days to cultivate a new habit. Now there is growing evidence in neuropsychology to support that belief. It appears twenty-one days is the approximate time required for the development of new neural pathways in your brain. For this reason I have set up this program so each section focuses on a particular principle for a minimum of three weeks.

In addition, I have provided three powerful tools that support different aspects of each principle. If you did nothing more than work solely with these tools, your life would greatly improve. Combine the tools with the principles and your life will never be the same.

There are three ways you might choose to do this program:

1. **The Whole Enchilada.** If you do each section of the program consecutively, it will cover a span of fifteen weeks. This is great if you have the time to commit to such intensive focus and if you like this type of structure.

2. **Bite-Sized Chunks.** If you find a fifteen-week commitment too long or undesirable, choose to do one three-week section at a time.

3. **Pick and Choose.** Some people are simply not suited for structured programs. If you know that's true for you, feel free to choose the exercises and aspects of the program that appeal most to you.

It's difficult to design a program that will work for everyone. What I've given you is only a guideline. If you know up front that if you have to journal you won't do the program, then instead of journaling do a mental review. If you find you need more than three weeks to complete a section, by all means, take the time needed.

This program is for *you*. Allow yourself the flexibility to alter the schedule and to pace yourself as it works best for you.

INTEGRATING THE
FIRST PRINCIPLE

Nothing Has to Happen My Way

WEEK 1

Nothing Has to Happen My Way

DAILY

➤ Read the ***First Principle Affirmation*** aloud. This is a powerful way of setting your daily intention and will help to create thoughts throughout the day that support this principle.

➤ Repeat the ***First Principle*** to yourself *every time* a negative emotion emerges in you. This trains your brain to run your life experiences consistently through the filter of that principle.

➤ Keep the ***First Principle*** on your radar by using visual and auditory reminders.

➤ Do ***The Worry Eliminator*** exercise.

JOURNAL

➤ ***Journal a success*** you had in applying the First Principle today. How did a focus on this principle change your experience?

➤ Journal your experience today of your work with ***The Worry Eliminator***. How did letting go of something you had no control over affect your day?

FIRST PRINCIPLE AFFIRMATION

Nothing Has to Happen My Way

Wherever I go and whatever I do today, I choose to accept my current reality and to work with it to bring about the highest and best outcome. I take comfort in knowing nothing has to happen my way for me to be at peace.

I am grateful for this day and for the gifts that this day will bring me—whether they are easy-to-accept gifts or challenges. I accept what is and allow it without resistance.

I release my expectations and my assumptions. I choose to be in the present moment and am empowered by knowing that my well-being is not determined by what is happening around me.

I take responsibility for creating peace within me and embrace my ability to adapt and be flexible in situations where it is needed.

I seek to empower, rather than disempower others, and to be mindful of situations where my power can be misused.

I open myself to accepting what I cannot change and release my need for anything to be different from the way it is.

I choose to see what is right and good in every situation—rather than what is not.

THE WORRY ELIMINATOR

Tool #1

This simple but effective exercise is designed to enable you to do two things: divert your energy and focus to the things you *do* have control over, and release a disempowering pattern of focusing on what is outside your control. Both will increase your sense of personal empowerment.

Take a few minutes and think of the things you worry about. *Write each worry under one of the two categories listed below.* If the situation is something you can bring change to, place it under "Can Control." If it's something you have no control over, place it under "Cannot Control."

Now take each item listed on the right side, read it aloud, and say, "I release you." Take your time and fully commit to your statement. If the worry later reappears and vies again for your attention, repeat the statement. Be stubbornly persistent. By doing so, you extinguish old neural pathways and create new ones by focusing on areas of your life where positive changes can be made.

Record your experience using this exercise in your journal.

Can Control	Cannot Control

WEEK 2

Nothing Has to Happen My Way

DAILY

- ➢ Continue to read the *First Principle Affirmation* aloud.

- ➢ Keep the *First Principle* on your radar by repeating it to yourself often. Use visual and auditory reminders.

- ➢ Do the *Releasing and Replacing Negative Beliefs* exercise.

JOURNAL

- ➢ *Journal a success* you had in applying the First Principle today.

- ➢ Journal your experience today of your work with *Releasing and Replacing Negative Beliefs*. How did replacing a negative belief affect your experience of the stressful event?

RELEASING AND REPLACING NEGATIVE BELIEFS

Tool #2

The goal of this exercise is to release negative beliefs that continue to bring you pain. When you replace them with healthier versions, your emotions will change in positive ways.

Think about an area of your life—your work, your primary relationship, your family, your children, etc.—that triggers a negative emotion. Write down the upsetting *thought* you have in that particular circumstance in the template below.

"**I release myself from the belief that** _____(the thought)_____ **and the** _____(emotion)_____ **it creates because nothing has to happen my way for me to be at peace.**"

Next, look at the list below and choose the emotion you feel in this instance:

- ➤ Anger
- ➤ Sadness
- ➤ Fear
- ➤ Resentment
- ➤ Worry
- ➤ Frustration
- ➤ Agitation

> ➢ Guilt
> ➢ Anxiety
> ➢ Shame
> ➢ Other_____

Now write down the upsetting *emotion* you have. As an illustration, if I'm angry because my boss didn't give me a raise and I think it's unfair, then my example would read like this:

"I release myself from the belief that it's unfair that my boss didn't give me a raise **and from the** anger **it creates because nothing has to happen my way for me to be at peace."**

Other examples:

"I release myself from the belief that my friend should care enough about me to call periodically to see how I'm doing **and the** sadness **it creates because nothing has to happen my way for me to be at peace."**

"I release myself from the belief that I need to weigh fifteen pounds less **and the** shame **it creates because nothing has to happen my way for me to be at peace."**

When you have completed your statement by filling in the thought and emotion, *read it aloud and imagine releasing it.* Finally, replace the old belief with a statement that is healthier and brings you greater well-being. This is important because an old belief will not be released unless there is a replacement for it. Using the example of your boss not giving you a raise, a replacement might be:

"My boss did not give me a raise. I wanted a raise but nothing has to happen my way for me to be at peace. I am grateful for my job and will ask what I can do to better position myself for a raise."

This active process of rerouting your belief patterns is an excellent way to personalize the First Principle: Nothing Has to Happen My Way.

WEEK 3

Nothing Has to Happen My Way

DAILY

➤ Continue to read the **First Principle Affirmation** aloud.

➤ Repeat the **First Principle** to yourself anytime a negative thought or emotion surfaces.

➤ Do the **Dissolving Ingrained Beliefs** exercise.

JOURNAL

➤ **Journal a success** you had in applying the First Principle today. How did your response today differ from previous ones in similar situations because of using this principle?

➤ Journal your experience today of your work with **Dissolving Ingrained Beliefs**. How did aligning yourself with love affect the belief you were trying to dissolve?

DISSOLVING INGRAINED BELIEFS

Tool #3

What happens when you turn on a light in a dark room? The room suddenly fills with light and the darkness magically disappears. Darkness and light cannot coexist, for in light's presence darkness has no life.

The same is true with *love* and *fear*. Fear resides in the absence of love, but in love's presence fear cannot have life. Because love is the highest function of energy in this world, it is to our great advantage to align with it. When we do that we harness the power of love, which brings us a sense of abundant well-being.

Dissolving Ingrained Beliefs is a powerful exercise that retrains your brain by taking a deeply ingrained belief—one you don't want anymore such as "I am stupid," "I am not enough," "I am a failure," etc.—and holding it side by side with love. A dear friend of mine posted a passage on his blog that speaks beautifully to the power of love:

> *When I first encountered J.K. Rowling's description of a dementor attack, I was stunned to see how much it sounded like a description of these attacks of depression: like all happiness has been sucked out from within me and for several miles around, like it was just one endless stretch of bleakness. The depiction of the dementors themselves as dark, hooded creatures gliding soundlessly over their victims struck me as the best allegory for how*

these phases of depression crawled over me. The wizards in the Harry Potter books conjure the Patronus Charm to defend themselves from the dementors. What a wizard is required to do to conjure a strong Patronus is to seek refuge in his or her memories of happiness and love and cast the charm from there. The dementors, in J.K. Rowling's imagination, cannot withstand the power of even the remembrance of love and happiness.[12]

To conjure your Patronus, the power of love within you, begin by relaxing your breathing. Breathe with your diaphragm and place your hand on your abdomen so you can feel it moving up and down with each breath. As you do this, visualize a brilliant, white light filling up every cell of your body. Fill your heart first, then radiate the light out throughout your entire chest. Continue to breathe in that white light until it eventually fills your entire body. When your body can hold no more, envision the light spilling out through the pores of your skin until you're completely surrounded by it. Continue to breathe slowly and fully.

Now think of a time when you felt very much loved. What was it that created the feeling of love? Which person or persons were involved? Allow yourself to breathe in the memory of that feeling.

Bring to mind the sounds in this special memory. Was someone talking with you? Was there music, were birds chirping, or were other sounds involved? Breathe in the memory of those sounds.

Are there smells associated with this memory? Any fragrances or foods? If so, breathe in the memory of those smells.

Now, as you fully immerse yourself in the love of that comforting memory, bring to mind a fearful belief you want to extinguish.

Holding the loving memory you have brought to mind, place the fearful belief directly in front of you and see it as the darkness of fear that it is. As you allow the light to extend from you and move beyond you, allow the belief to dissolve in the light of your love, just as darkness does in the presence of light.

Finally, replace the belief with the following thoughts:

I am created in the image and likeness of God.
I am a being of light and love in this world.
I do not identify with fear and I release it as the mirage it is.

This exercise empowers you by creating a conscious alignment with love. A disempowering human belief cannot prevail when you are embodying the energy of love. Each time you do this exercise, you diminish the power fear has in your life and expose it as a lie. Repeat this exercise daily until the belief is nothing more than a faint memory.

INTEGRATING THE
SECOND PRINCIPLE

Everything Matters

WEEK 1

Everything Matters

DAILY

➢ Read the **Second Principle Affirmation** aloud. This is a powerful way of setting your daily intention and will help to create thoughts throughout the day that support this principle.

➢ As a proactive measure, keep the **Second Principle** on your radar by repeating it to yourself as often as you can remember. This is not done in *response* to anything but rather as a way to recharge the new neural pathway being created.

➢ Do the **Tracking Your Successes** exercise.

JOURNAL

➢ **Journal a success** you had today in applying the Second Principle. How did a focus on this principle change your experience today?

➢ Journal your experience today of your work with **Tracking Your Successes**. How did keeping a list of steps you took toward your goals affect you?

SECOND PRINCIPLE AFFIRMATION

Everything Matters

Every thought I think, every word I speak, and everything I do matters. I seek to make good choices and to be guided by the power of love in every instance.

I claim my ability to respond with love rather than with fearful reaction. With a loving intent, I seek to be the clearest and most loving communicator I can be and when I am not, I will offer an apology.

I acknowledge the ripple effect of my actions and strive for impeccability in all my affairs. Right action strengthens not only me, but others as well.

I release my focus on that which is negative in my life and the lives of others. I choose to see what is working and to amplify it.

I ask for wisdom in establishing healthy boundaries for myself and for clear communication of them to others.

I choose to assume the best of others when I'm confused by their actions or troubled by their behavior. I release them from my judgment and I walk with a forgiving heart, for I recognize we are all on a journey of learning.

I seek to do the best I can—where I am—with what I have this day. I ask that the fullest potential in me be activated in all I do.

TRACKING YOUR SUCCESSES

Tool #4

This exercise is listed under the Second Principle because of the importance of acknowledging your successes. Claiming successes gives you a sense of accomplishment, increases your optimism, and gives you confidence as you make progress toward your goals. As you focus on what works in your life rather than what does not, your trust in yourself and in the Universe will increase.

Small, successful steps eventually bring big successes. The more you recognize your successes, no matter how small, the more you will be able to trust that you can create what you want in life by reaching your goals.

Goals can be physical, emotional, mental, or spiritual. A *physical* goal might be eating smaller meals more frequently during the day. An *emotional* goal could be releasing judgment of a coworker. Doing sudoku for thirty minutes each day could constitute a *mental* goal. A *spiritual* goal might consist of asking the Universe for what you want and documenting the results.

Make a list of the goals you choose and keep a daily log of your successes and the positive steps you take toward them. Write these down daily in your journal. Pat yourself on the back and give yourself credit for making them happen. Be your own best cheerleader, soaking up the good feelings that come as you savor the experiences of your success.

WEEK 2

Everything Matters

DAILY

➤ Continue to read the *Second Principle Affirmation* aloud.

➤ Keep the *Second Principle* on your radar by repeating it to yourself often. Use visual and auditory reminders.

➤ Familiarize yourself with *Making Effective Apologies* and look for an opportunity to make an apology this week.

JOURNAL

➤ *Journal a success* you had today in applying the Second Principle. How did a focus on this principle change your experience today?

➤ *Write down any apologies* made during the week, whether they were done in person, by phone, or in writing. Note your experience of giving the apology as well as the response of the recipient.

MAKING EFFECTIVE APOLOGIES

Tool #5

Apologies heal. An effective apology says you are sorry for the pain you have caused and comes with a promise to do your best not to offend the person in the same way again. The key components of an effective apology are:

1. **I am sorry** (taking responsibility)
2. **I hurt you** (the impact)
3. **by** _____ (the specific behavior)
4. **I will do my best never to do it again** (the commitment)

As previously discussed, apologies are *not* restricted to those times when you clearly did something wrong. Apologies are warranted whenever you do or say something that creates pain in another, regardless of your good intent or the absence of wrongdoing.

Using the steps above, an apology might be: "I'm sorry I hurt you by sharing that information. I promise never to assume I can share personal information without asking you first. Please forgive me."

Another version: "I'm so sorry I communicated in a way that hurt your feelings. I love you and never want to hurt you. How can I make this right?"

Think of three people to whom you owe apologies for your past actions. Choose one of them to offer either a written or verbal apology that contains the four steps listed above.

WEEK 3

Everything Matters

DAILY

> ➤ Continue to read the *Second Principle Affirmation* aloud.

> ➤ Keep the *Second Principle* on your radar by repeating it to yourself often.

> ➤ Do the *Simplify/Amplify* exercise.

JOURNAL

> ➤ *Journal a success* you had today in applying the Second Principle. How did a focus on this principle change your experience today?

> ➤ Journal every step you take that moves you toward accomplishing your stated goals of *simplifying and amplifying*.

SIMPLIFY/AMPLIFY

Tool #6

Many of us feel overwhelmed by the ever-increasing rate of change in our lives. Bombarded by the endless influx of new information, we become stressed by the strain of keeping up with it all. Our lives become filled with commitments and obligations we no longer care about but often continue simply because they are familiar to us. Slowly but surely we can create lives that are far cries from what we truly desire.

Simplify/Amplify is a valuable exercise for taking stock of what you no longer need in your life and for creating more of what you value. This exercise consists of making two lists that can be as long or as short as suits your needs.

The first is a list of things that will simplify your life. This might include things you want to eliminate such as clutter in your house, or a book club you no longer enjoy. It can also include things you want to do less of, like eating sugar or spending so much time online.

The second list will consist of things you want to spend more time doing such as being aware of gratitudes or cooking your own meals.

Here is an example of a Simplify/Amplify list:

SIMPLIFY

- Watch less TV
- Outsource some home repairs
- Decrease internet surfing
- Spend less time playing computer games
- Decrease my number of commitments

AMPLIFY

- Increase quality time with my spouse
- Have more play time with others
- Connect spiritually when I wake up each morning
- Organize my home office
- Improve my money management

After creating your lists, circle two items on your "Simplify" list that you're willing to commit to doing less of and circle two items on your "Amplify" list you're willing to give more time to.

This exercise can quickly improve the quality of your life. As you simplify your life by releasing what you no longer want or want less of, you free up time to amplify more of what you do want!

INTEGRATING THE
THIRD PRINCIPLE

Greater Is That Which Is within Me

WEEK 1

Greater Is That Which Is within Me

DAILY

➤ Read the **Third Principle Affirmation** aloud. This is a powerful way of setting your daily intention and will help to create thoughts throughout the day that support this principle.

➤ Repeat the **Third Principle** to yourself as often as you can remember. This is not done in *response* to anything but rather as a way to recharge the new neural pathway being created.

➤ Do **The Five-Minute Meditation** exercise.

JOURNAL

➤ **Journal a success** you had today in applying the Third Principle. How did a focus on this principle change your experience today?

➤ Journal your experience today of your work with **The Five-Minute Meditation**. What effect did this exercise have on you?

THIRD PRINCIPLE AFFIRMATION

Greater Is That Which Is within Me

I begin this day with the recognition that my connection with my greater self is greater than anything outside of me.

I give myself the timeless experience of being in the precious now. Like a dolphin filling its lungs with life-giving oxygen as it comes to the surface, I will connect within for renewal during my day so I am centered and balanced.

I choose to honor my greater self by making time to align with it. I will step off the merry-go-round of constant activity so my perspective is clear and my choices are in alignment with right action.

As I go forth this day, I choose to see through the eyes of my greater self and ask for guidance. I commit to *seeing* what is needed and to *being* what is needed so I may be an expression of love and positive action in the world.

I will direct energy in the form of prayer to those people and situations that come into my awareness, letting go of my version of what I think would be the best outcome by sending healing and wholeness for the highest good of all.

I claim the power I have to express love and will joyfully look for those moments when I can express it.

THE FIVE-MINUTE MEDITATION[13]

Tool #7

The Five-Minute Meditation is a remarkable tool for learning to create an inner connection and learning to trust that connection. Choose a quiet place and begin by sitting in a comfortable, erect position with some support for your back if needed. Relax your body as much as possible while retaining your posture. Bring the center of your attention within by focusing on your breath or visualizing a scene that helps you calm your body and mind. Allow about thirty seconds for this.

Active Portion

Make an affirmation such as "This is the active part of my meditation, and I ask my higher self to help me become aware of where love is needed." Then simply wait and listen. When thoughts of people or projects or worries about your life situation or your daily activities arise, don't dwell on them. Simply convert them into the most positive thought-forms you can formulate at the time, then release them. The way you find yourself doing it is the right way for you to do it. Devote two to two and a half minutes to this.

Passive Portion

Next affirm, "Now I begin the passive part of my meditation, and I ask my higher self to provide me with the energy and wisdom I need at this point in my life." Again, wait and listen, but when thoughts arise during this time, try to simply observe them and let them go. Allow about the same amount of time for the passive period as for the active one, for a total meditation time of about five minutes. During this time try to be as open as possible and remember that much of what takes place here happens quickly once you attain this openness. It may also happen largely below the level of consciousness.

In using this approach, realize you are turning control of the process over to your inner wisdom—and trust it. Trust yourself to give yourself what you need and try to let the process unfold naturally, without forcing.

Steps for the Five-Minute Meditation

1. Relax and bring your focus of attention within yourself for about thirty seconds.

2. Affirm to yourself the purpose of active meditation and practice it for about two minutes.

3. Do the same for passive meditation.

4. Thank yourself for giving yourself this time.

WEEK 2

Greater Is That Which Is within Me

DAILY
- ➤ Continue to read the ***Third Principle Affirmation*** aloud.

- ➤ Keep the ***Third Principle*** on your radar by repeating it to yourself often. Use visual and auditory reminders.

- ➤ Do the ***Morning and Night*** exercise.

JOURNAL
- ➤ ***Journal a success*** you had today in applying the Third Principle. How did a focus on this principle change your experience today?

- ➤ Journal your experience today of your work with ***Morning and Night***. What impact did starting and ending your day in this manner have upon you?

MORNING AND NIGHT

Tool #8

Starting your day with affirming thoughts and loving action can have a profoundly positive effect upon your well-being. Try this exercise to see what the benefits are for you.

Morning

When you wake up, your brain has not yet kicked into analytical mode. This transition time is a perfect opportunity to direct or send love to those in need:

- ➢ Send loving thoughts to someone you are grateful for.

- ➢ Send loving thoughts to someone who is difficult for you to deal with.

- ➢ Send loving thoughts to someone in need.

- ➢ Say, "I love you" to yourself.

Night

Many people have difficulty turning off their thoughts when they lie down to sleep. This exercise can be very helpful because it allows your mind to relax enough for your body to move easily into sleep. It's a conscious recognition of your daily personal growth and a beautiful way to complete each day.

At bedtime ask yourself these questions:

> ➤ "What were my gifts today?" As you review them, give gratitude to yourself and the Universe for them.

> ➤ "What were my successes?" Claim your accomplishments and give gratitude.

> ➤ "Where did I give love and what was the impact of doing so?" Pat yourself on the back for creating those experiences.

Acknowledge that you are a Being of light and love with a connection to the greater Universe. Breathe in the energy of love, allowing it to fill every cell of your body. Let yourself bask in that energy—and sleep.

WEEK 3

Greater Is That Which Is within Me

DAILY

➤ Continue to read the ***Third Principle Affirmation*** aloud.

➤ Keep the ***Third Principle*** on your radar by repeating it to yourself often.

➤ Do the ***Rebalancing*** exercise twice a day.

JOURNAL

➤ ***Journal a success*** you had today in applying the Third Principle. How did a focus on this principle change your experience?

➤ Journal your experience today of your work with ***Rebalancing***. How did creating the space for internal balance change your experience today?

REBALANCING

Tool #9

Far too often we feel as though we're on a hamster wheel. One way to create internal balance is to give ourselves a few minutes to step away from the constant mental and physical activity in our lives.

We often resist this because our lives are full and we make the case that there is always something more important to do. Yet what could be more valuable than rebalancing your entire system? Creating balance nourishes your physical body, allows your mind to disengage, soothes your emotions, and engages your spiritual self.

At least twice a day, give yourself the gift of creating a space where you can close your eyes and become the observer of your experience. Instead of doing—*be*. Set your worries and concerns temporarily aside, allowing your breathing to slow. Let yourself gently shift into the peacefulness of the moment and experience the tranquility of your greater self.

INTEGRATING THE FOURTH PRINCIPLE

Be the Miracle

WEEK 1

Be the Miracle

DAILY

➢ Read the ***Fourth Principle Affirmation*** aloud. This is a powerful way of setting your daily intention and will help to create thoughts throughout the day that support this principle.

➢ Repeat the ***Fourth Principle*** to yourself as often as you can—not in *response* to anything but as a way to recharge the new neural pathway being created.

➢ Do the ***Five Daily Gratitudes*** exercise.

JOURNAL

➢ ***Journal a success*** you had today in applying the Fourth Principle. How did a focus on this principle change your experience?

➢ Journal your experience today of your work with ***Five Daily Gratitudes***. What effect did this exercise have on you?

FOURTH PRINCIPLE AFFIRMATION

Be the Miracle

I open myself to the wonder of this day and to seeing the miracles that surround me.

I am a living miracle of love. I choose to function today as love by being what is needed.

As I go through this day, I will focus on what is working and be filled with gratitude for the abundance in my life.

I choose to be a miracle today by functioning at my highest in every situation.

I commit to giving others recognition and being respectful in all my communications.

I choose to see others today through fresh eyes. I release any former judgments that keep me from experiencing them as they are today.

I choose happiness by focusing on what is working in my life and by seeing the miracles that surround me.

If I fall short today, I will embrace my effort rather than judging the stumble.

I choose to be a living example of doing the best I can, wherever I am, with what I have.

FIVE DAILY GRATITUDES

Tool #10

List five things you are grateful for each day. That's all—just five things. It's such a simple exercise, but oh what a powerful one! It's so easy to become numb to the many good things in our lives and to stop being grateful for them. As long as they remain undisturbed, our tendency is to let them slip out of our awareness. Listing five gratitudes a day reactivates our awareness through consciously focusing on our blessings.

As you make your list, if you find you're running out of gratitudes to write down, you're probably thinking too broadly and listing categories instead of experiences. For example, listing "health," "work," "family," "friends," and "pets" will quickly exhaust anyone's pool of gratitudes. But those are categories. Instead, look within those categories for specific experiences.

Some specific examples of gratitude might include: a "thank you" received from your boss on Monday morning; a good hair day; a hug from a coworker; remembering to pick up a special gift; a gift you received; the availability of fresh food; or working out when you didn't feel like it.

This exercise will show you the many gifts in your life and sharpen your sense of the things that are working well. It will train you to have a positive focus. Here's how it works:

➢   Being grateful for the abundance in your life draws more abundance to you.

➢   More abundance gives you greater confidence in your ability to manifest what you want in your life.

➢   Greater confidence increases the likelihood of more successes.

➢   Those successes, in turn, create more abundance and the positive cycle continues.

By keeping a record of five gratitudes a day for thirty days, you will have listed 150 gratitudes in only a month! Consistently expressing gratitude creates a positive loop that only gets better over time.

WEEK 2

Be the Miracle

DAILY

- ➤ Continue to read the *Fourth Principle Affirmation* aloud.

- ➤ Keep the *Fourth Principle* on your radar by repeating it to yourself often. Use visual and auditory reminders.

- ➤ Do the *Seeing a Daily Miracle* exercise.

JOURNAL

- ➤ *Journal a success* you had today in applying the Fourth Principle. How did a focus on this principle change your experience?

- ➤ Journal your experience today of your work with *Seeing a Daily Miracle*. How much effort did it take to see a miracle today? Did you see more than one?

SEEING A DAILY MIRACLE

Tool #11

In truth, all of life is a miracle—whether we're examining a leaf, watching a kitten play with yarn, or appreciating the magic of our bodies' complexity. Miracles are easy to see if we train ourselves *to look for them.* Here is a wonderful practice I encourage you to do for twenty-one days so that seeing miracles becomes an ingrained habit.

Take a sheet of lined paper and number it from one to twenty-one. Place it in a very visible area such as on a mirror, refrigerator, or kitchen cabinet. Keeping it in sight makes it easier to remember as you go about your day. Begin each of the twenty-one days with the intent of seeing a miracle, and when you do, make sure you write it down on your paper.

Making a list of miracles will bring magic to your life and will also expand your list of gratitudes. You might say something like, "As I begin this day, I open myself to recognizing a miracle and being grateful for it." This sets up your anticipation of a miracle and will often heighten your focus, which will aid in your effort.

Hope and positivity abound when we train ourselves to see miracles.

WEEK 3

Be the Miracle

DAILY

- ➤ Continue to read the *Fourth Principle Affirmation* aloud.

- ➤ Keep the *Fourth Principle* on your radar by repeating it to yourself often.

- ➤ Begin the *List of Wonders* exercise.

JOURNAL

- ➤ *Journal a success* you had today in applying the Fourth Principle. How did a focus on this principle change your experience?

- ➤ Journal your experience today of your work with *A List of Wonders*. What was the effect of recalling special moments in your life?

A LIST OF WONDERS

Tool #12

There are thousands of magical moments in a life. Many of them are made up of first experiences with something new. However, after the novelty has passed, the magic often escapes us. It was exhilarating the first time I put my head underwater in a swimming pool. A year later it was routine. How tragic it is to grow numb through familiarity to life's wondrous moments.

One of the reasons children are so stimulating to be around is because life is a constant discovery for them, with an ongoing array of first experiences. Many grandparents can attest that witnessing their grandchildren's delightful reactions reawakens their own sense of wonder.

This particular exercise, however, does not require you to have grandchildren or to spend time with them. It consists of remembering and recapturing the magic of your most precious moments in life.

As I began my own list, I was amazed by how many delightful experiences I could remember. I've listed some of them, many of which were first experiences. This list is only a smattering of over 200 special moments I listed over a two-week period.

Smelling my hands after rubbing the green covering of a walnut
Standing outside in a summer downpour
Dancing until I could barely stand
Floating underwater in a swimming pool

Making taffy with my mother
Getting my first haircut at a barber shop
Listening to a live symphony
Skinny dipping with my friends
Making mud pies with my brother and sisters
Watching fireworks streak across the night sky
Using tin cans with twine strung between them as a telephone
Watching fireflies on a warm, summer evening
Smelling Vicks VapoRub as my mom massaged it into my chest
Carving a cave in a huge snowdrift with my father
Watching lightning dance across the sky
Listening to steady rainfall while lying in a tent
Watching the sun set over the ocean
Sitting by a campfire and roasting marshmallows
Lighting my first wooden match
Jumping on a trampoline
Riding a bicycle for the first time
Finger painting on the kitchen table
Petting a kangaroo
Watching ants hard at work
Watching a hummingbird hover over a flower
My first kiss with my wife
Riding a Ferris wheel
Blowing dandelion seeds
Biting into a lemon
Holding a baby bird
Being tickled by my father
Flying a kite
Holding a newborn baby

Making a snow angel
Watching the flickering flame of a single candle
Blowing soap bubbles
Skipping rocks across a stream with my buddies

Get the picture? *Rekindle the miracle of life by writing down some of your most memorable moments each day. After listing them, close your eyes and relive them. Savor the memory by allowing yourself to re-experience the joy and delight you felt at that time.* I think you'll be pleasantly surprised by the results as you give yourself time to reminisce.

By reconnecting with the best in your past, you build a bridge to an ongoing experience of gratitude for the many wonders that currently make your life a miracle.

INTEGRATING THE
FIFTH PRINCIPLE

I Surrender My Humanness

WEEK 1

I Surrender My Humanness

DAILY

➢ Read the ***Fifth Principle Affirmation*** aloud. This is a powerful way of setting your daily intention. It will help to create thoughts throughout the day that support this principle.

➢ Keep the ***Fifth Principle*** on your radar by repeating it to yourself as often as you can remember to do so. This is not done in *response* to anything but rather as a way to recharge the new neural pathway being created.

➢ Do the ***Better and Brighter*** exercise.

JOURNAL

➢ ***Journal a success*** you had today in applying the Fifth Principle. How did a focus on this principle change your experience today?

➢ Journal your experience today of your work with ***Better and Brighter***. What was the effect on the other person whose day you made better and brighter? How did it affect you?

FIFTH PRINCIPLE AFFIRMATION

I Surrender My Humanness

I choose to give what is needed rather than focusing solely on what I need.

I recognize and embrace the interconnectedness of all life.

I surrender my humanness to flow with that which is for the highest good in every situation I encounter today.

I surrender my humanness by releasing any fear surrounding money, my body, or my relationships.

I surrender to my greater self and welcome its guidance.

I free myself from continued pain by letting go of judgment and forgiving those who have hurt me.

I endeavor to be the person I want to see in the world by thinking, speaking, and acting with love as my guide.

BETTER AND BRIGHTER

Tool #13

Consciously choosing to make someone's day better and brighter is a very powerful exercise for putting love into action. This exercise is *premeditated*. It's not just being friendly with people; it's a step up from that.

For example, casually chatting with the grocery clerk is a friendly thing to do. However, approaching the checkout counter with the *intent* of making the clerk's day better and brighter by expressing gratitude for her service will likely bring about a deeper connection. This might entail complimenting her on how well she does her job or how much you appreciate her friendly smile and demeanor.

You can also make someone's day better and brighter anonymously. An anonymous gift is special for the giver *and* the receiver. For the giver it's an act of surrendering humanness, because there is no personal recognition to stroke the ego. For the recipient, it can be a rare and unique experience, validating that one is loved. Knowing someone cares can restore a lost faith in humanity.

Here are some ideas for making someone's day better and brighter:

- ➤ Look for an opportunity to give a compliment.
- ➤ Send an e-card to express thanks.
- ➤ Give recognition to another who has helped you.
- ➤ Smile at someone you don't know.

> ➤ Express your appreciation for another's kindness.
> ➤ Send money anonymously.
> ➤ Compliment others on their appearance.
> ➤ Encourage someone who is discouraged.
> ➤ Offer your place to another person standing in line.
> ➤ Help a friend with outdoor work, errands, or organizing a closet.
> ➤ Give away something another might find useful.

Make a daily effort to consciously make someone's day better and brighter. Pay attention to the person's reaction and the effect it has upon you.

WEEK 2

I Surrender My Humanness

DAILY

➤ Continue to read the **Fifth Principle Affirmation** aloud.

➤ Keep the **Fifth Principle** on your radar by repeating it to yourself often. Use visual and auditory reminders.

➤ Do the **Finding Meaning in the Mundane** exercise.

JOURNAL

➤ **Journal a success** you had today in applying the Fifth Principle. How did a focus on this principle change your experience today?

➤ Journal your experience today of your work with **Finding Meaning in the Mundane**. How did giving meaning to an everyday activity change it for you?

FINDING MEANING IN THE MUNDANE

Tool #14

We tend to compartmentalize our spiritual practice in Western culture, often relegating it to our attendance at churches, temples, and synagogues. It's generally not as interwoven with our daily life as it is in many Eastern cultures. However, with only a slight adjustment in our mindset, we can easily transform normal daily activities into meaningful spiritual experiences.

Taking out the trash, cooking a meal, paying bills, taking a shower, cleaning eyeglasses, watering flowers—these are mundane activities for most of us. We do them out of necessity and very often without thought.

With a slight adjustment in the way we approach them, these daily activities can be used as opportunities to express gratitude, to send healing energy to others, or to manifest what we want to create in our lives. Here are a few examples of ways to find meaning in mundane tasks:

Taking out the trash. As you wheel the trash to the curb, ask that the trash from your life be released in the form of negative thoughts, items no longer needed, and unhealthy patterns.

Cooking meals. Express gratitude for all who have made it possible for the food to make its way to your kitchen. That includes the growers, harvesters, shippers, and grocers. Send blessings to them all. As you prepare your food, fill it with love and ask that those who eat it be physically nourished by it.

Paying bills. Paying those who have provided services is an act of gratitude. Express your gratitude for the wonder and convenience of electricity, water, cell phones, and Internet service. Write "thank you" on the checks you write to pay your bills. It's a way of expressing gratitude for the services you've received.

Taking a shower. Be aware of the joy of bathing in heated water. As the water pours over your body, ask that your judgments of others and all unloving thoughts be washed down the drain.

Cleaning eyeglasses. When cleaning your eyeglasses or washing a window, claim your desire to see clearly where love is needed that day—for yourself and others. Ask for clarity in your perceptions and to see your day through the eyes of love.

Watering flowers or shrubs. As you nourish the roots of your plants with water, reflect on the ways you are nourished in your life. What are you doing that feeds you? What can you do to take better care of yourself?

The possibilities are endless! Almost every task we do can be made sacred and meaningful if we frame it with a spiritual intent. *Be creative and write down three ways you can bring meaning to mundane actions in your life. Try them out and journal your experience.*

WEEK 3

I Surrender My Humanness

DAILY

➤ Continue to read the *Fifth Principle Affirmation* aloud.

➤ Keep the *Fifth Principle* on your radar by repeating it to yourself often.

➤ Do the *My Magnificent Day* exercise.

JOURNAL

➤ *Journal a success* you had today in applying the Fifth Principle. How did a focus on this principle change your experience today?

➤ Journal your experience today of your work with *My Magnificent Day*. Write down everything you did to make it so.

MY MAGNIFICENT DAY

Tool #15

My Magnificent Day is a one-day activity where the goal is to consistently look for the positive aspects in everything you do and experience. Many of the previous exercises help to make this one possible. A magnificent day can be created by keeping a positive focus, being grateful, seeing the miracles, and being fully in the present moment.

This exercise can change your life. Although my clients report many gifts from doing this exercise, the epiphany comes when they discover they can *choose* to make a single day magnificent. It shows them how much power they actually have in creating their experiences. regardless of what's happening around them. As a result, their sense of personal empowerment increases significantly.

The exercise starts with the intent that *this is going to be a magnificent day.* Stating this powerful intent is key and begins the creation process by aligning your thoughts with that intent. Steadfastly maintaining that focus throughout the day creates a magnificent day as your reality.

Keep a piece of paper handy and jot down every experience that makes your day magnificent. At the end of the day, review your list and think about what you did that made it so. What did you do differently from what you typically do? What did it require of you?

My Magnificent Day shows us the power we have to shape our positive experiences of life. If one day can be made magnificent purely through our desire to make it so, then we have the capability of doing it much more consistently.

EPILOGUE

You deserve to be happy and to experience the best version of you. As you work with The Five Principles, be persistent. Be *very* persistent. Every day matters and every step counts. Changing patterns to transform your life takes practice, for it is indeed a process. It helps a lot to consistently acknowledge the positive steps you have taken.

Each of us is the light and the hope of the world. As we awaken and shine, we show others it can be done. We give them hope. Through functioning as the love we are, we manifest love upon this physical earth, making it possible to fulfill our destinies both individually and collectively. The world has never been more ready, and our good choices have never been more needed.

As you journey forward with these Five Principles as your guide, may you be empowered by knowing you are a part of it all. May you see the miracles in your life and be a miracle in the lives of others.

I am you. You are me. We are one.

NOTES

1. *Flourish: A Visionary New Understanding of Happiness and Well-being,* Martin E. P. Seligman, Free Press, 2012.

2. Used with permission of Kandy Miller.

3. Edward Stanley, 3rd Earl of Derby, Speech in 1873.

4. Used with permission of EarthLight, Inc.

5. *Loving What Is: Four Questions That Can Change Your Life,* Byron Katie with Stephen Mitchell, Harmony Books, 2002.

6. Compiled from numerous online sources.

7. Albert Einstein.

8. Pierre Teilhard de Chardin.

9. Jelaluddin Rumi.

10. Heraclitus of Ephesus, a Greek philosopher (c. 535 BC–475 BC).

11. *Buddha's Brain: the practical neuroscience of happiness, love & wisdom,* Rick Hanson with Richard Mendius, 1999.

12. Used with permission of Aniruddhan Vasudevan.

13. Created by and used with permission of EarthLight, Inc.

CONNECT WITH THE AUTHOR

Sign up at **StevenSmith-author.com** to be placed on my mailing list. In return you'll receive a free bi-monthly newsletter with articles of interest and updates of future publications. You'll also find numerous ways to connect with me on my website through the following social media:

- ➢ Facebook
- ➢ Twitter
- ➢ Google+
- ➢ LinkedIn
- ➢ YouTube
- ➢ Pinterest

Let's stay in touch,

Steven

Made in the USA
Monee, IL
17 November 2020